Practical Tips for
Turners & Carvers

Practical Tips for
Turners & Carvers

THE BEST FROM
WOODTURNING MAGAZINE
WOODCarving MAGAZINE

Guild of Master Craftsman Publications Ltd

First published in 1995 by
Guild of Master Craftsman Publications Ltd,
Castle Place, 166 High Street, Lewes, East Sussex BN7 1XU

ISBN 0 946819 91 2

Designed by GMC Design

Printed and bound in Great Britain by Eyre & Spottiswoode Ltd, Margate

Contents

PART 1: Woodturning Tips

SECTION 1   CHUCKS

SECTION 2   LATHES

SECTION 3   TOOLS

SECTION 4 TURNING TECHNIQUES

SECTION 5 SANDING & FINISHING

PART 2: Woodcarving Tips

SECTION 6 DRAWING & DESIGN

SECTION 7   SHARPENING

SECTION 8   TOOLS & TECHNIQUES

SECTION 9   VICES & WORKHOLDERS

SECTION 10 WOOD

SECTION 11 LETTERING

SECTION 12 FINISHING

Carving and turning are two of the oldest crafts, dating back to when man first started shaping wood. The shapes of chisels and gouges were perfected centuries ago, but there have been many changes in other areas, such as metallurgy, abrasives, work holding devices, and of course the introduction of electric power.

In turning this has of course meant powered lathes and equipment for power sanding, while in carving we have seen the introduction of flexible shaft machines with rotary grinding cutters, reciprocating carving heads, and carving discs on angle grinders. Both crafts have benefited from the use of power saws, such as bandsaws, chainsaws and table saws.

There is now a vast array of tools and equipment to choose from, which we welcome as a sign of increasing interest in the crafts. Tool tests in *Woodturning* and *Woodcarving* magazines will evaluate them and let you know how useful they are.

However, we know there are many hobby turners and carvers working on a limited budget – many are retired or unemployed. Necessity, and lack of funds being the mother of invention, has led many craftspeople to devise new methods, jigs and equipment to solve their problems.

This is where the Tips pages of our magazines have come from – the ingenuity of readers who have devised ways of doing things often with limited resources.

The tips in this book are drawn from both magazines. In the case of *Woodturning*, this is the second bumper bundle of bright ideas, whereas the carving tips are drawn from *Woodcarving* magazine since it started publication. We hope you will find all the tips useful and inspiring.

If you have any tips for your fellow turners and carvers, do write in and tell us about them – they could be published in our magazines and win you a cash prize as well.

Nick Hough, Editor *Woodturning*
Neil Bell, Editor *Woodcarving*

PART 1

Woodturning Tips

1 Chuck Brake

Like many turners, I have been in the habit of checking and stopping my chuck by hand after switching off the lathe. This was fine when I just used a Multistar chuck, but I recently bought a 4-jaw chuck. This has protruding jaws round the perimeter, making it very dangerous to try to stop by hand.

Not wishing to lose any fingers, I made a wooden hand brake which is contoured to fit round the rear part of the chuck. The inside of the contour is fitted with a leather strap. My lathe has twin bed bars, and the brake is pivoted round the furthest bar.

J.A. Trowell, 10 Old Farm Way, Oakland Park, Dawlish, Devon EX7 9SG.

2 Chuck from UPVC

To make a chuck from UPVC (to hold coasters etc. while finishing) I used a piece of scrap 56mm (2¼") thick cut to a cylinder of 102mm (4³/32") DIA on the bandsaw.

This was mounted on a screwchuck and a recess cut to fit my combination chuck of 86mm (3¼") DIA x 3mm (⅛") deep. It was then mounted on the combination chuck and hollowed to a depth of 4mm (5/32"), leaving a wall thickness of 4mm.

This was repeated a second time, giving two steps on the inside of the chuck, which was then hollowed out to a depth of 35mm (1³/8"), cutting into the side wall to give a slight bowl shape.

I cut a shallow groove in the side of the chuck 10mm (³/8") wide and 2mm (³/32") deep about 3mm (⅛") from the hollow end of the chuck. This groove takes a jubilee clip (or two joined by the screw thread) to give a compression on the finished jaws.

The chuck was then taken to the bandsaw and two cuts at right angles to each other were made to form the jaws. The cuts were made to the base of the hollow, from the open head of the chuck, and the jubilee clip then fitted.

I now had a chuck that would hold two sizes of coaster for finishing and decorating. So far, I have not had any slipping and there have not been any twirling bits of metal to snag the tools or fingers.

I used a 10mm (³/8") bedan throughout, but decorated the outsides with a fluted parting tool. This plastic chuck will last me a lifetime.

W.J. Pimlett, 52 Queen's Drive, Walton, Liverpool L4 6SH.

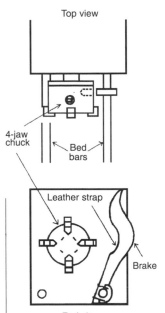

Top view

4-jaw chuck

Bed bars

Leather strap

Brake

End view

3 Colour coded 4-jaw

When, some time ago, I bought my APTC (Axminster) 4-jaw self centring scroll chuck, I found it was not always easy to read the jaw numbers or their corresponding slot numbers.

To overcome the problem I simply colour-coded each mating jaw and slot in highly coloured enamel paints. No 1 I coloured black, No 2 yellow, No 3 red, and No 4 green. They can all be easily identified, even in poor light.

A word of warning, however. All mating and sliding surfaces must be kept clean and free of paint or the chuck may not function smoothly. Paint must only be applied to the outside surfaces of the chuck body and jaws.

Davey Richardson, 8 Heath Rise, Fakenham, Norfolk NR21 8HU.

The same effect can be achieved by using small pieces of coloured sticky tape - Ed.

4 Indexing Ring with a Difference

Has any reader thought of using a lathe-mounted key-operated Jacobs chuck as an indexing ring? I've been using mine for some time, with very accurate results.

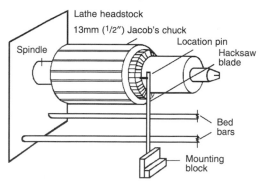

Lathe headstock
13mm (1/2") Jacob's chuck
Location pin
Spindle
Hacksaw blade
Bed bars
Mounting block

The toothed edge of the chuck where the key is normally engaged serves the same purpose as an indexing ring. Location is by a spring-loaded pin screwed to the lathe bed.

A hacksaw blade cut to the required length with the teeth ground off makes a suitable spring. The existing hole in one end of the hacksaw blade is used to take a bolt which is ground to a tight fit in one of the chuck indentations.

Although smaller than the average indexing plate, this device can be used to accurately locate any workpiece for spiral work, fluting, or any other task calling for a variety of dividing operations.

Small diameters can be fitted directly into the chuck and larger diameters accommodated between centres or on a backing plate mounted in the chuck.

My chuck has 30 indentations and a selection of locations are shown in the following table:

1 Chuck Brake

Like many turners, I have been in the habit of checking and stopping my chuck by hand after switching off the lathe. This was fine when I just used a Multistar chuck, but I recently bought a 4-jaw chuck. This has protruding jaws round the perimeter, making it very dangerous to try to stop by hand.

Not wishing to lose any fingers, I made a wooden hand brake which is contoured to fit round the rear part of the chuck. The inside of the contour is fitted with a leather strap. My lathe has twin bed bars, and the brake is pivoted round the furthest bar.

J.A. Trowell, 10 Old Farm Way, Oakland Park, Dawlish, Devon EX7 9SG.

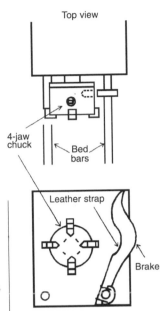

2 Chuck from UPVC

To make a chuck from UPVC (to hold coasters etc. while finishing) I used a piece of scrap 56mm (21/4") thick cut to a cylinder of 102mm (4³/32") DIA on the bandsaw.

This was mounted on a screwchuck and a recess cut to fit my combination chuck of 86mm (3¹/4") DIA x 3mm (¹/8") deep. It was then mounted on the combination chuck and hollowed to a depth of 4mm (⁵/32"), leaving a wall thickness of 4mm.

This was repeated a second time, giving two steps on the inside of the chuck, which was then hollowed out to a depth of 35mm (1³/8"), cutting into the side wall to give a slight bowl shape.

I cut a shallow groove in the side of the chuck 10mm (³/8") wide and 2mm (³/32") deep about 3mm (¹/8") from the hollow end of the chuck. This groove takes a jubilee clip (or two joined by the screw thread) to give a compression on the finished jaws.

The chuck was then taken to the bandsaw and two cuts at right angles to each other were made to form the jaws. The cuts were made to the base of the hollow, from the open head of the chuck, and the jubilee clip then fitted.

I now had a chuck that would hold two sizes of coaster for finishing and decorating. So far, I have not had any slipping and there have not been any twirling bits of metal to snag the tools or fingers.

I used a 10mm (³/8") bedan throughout, but decorated the outsides with a fluted parting tool. This plastic chuck will last me a lifetime.

W.J. Pimlett, 52 Queen's Drive, Walton, Liverpool L4 6SH.

3   Colour coded 4-jaw

When, some time ago, I bought my APTC (Axminster) 4-jaw self centring scroll chuck, I found it was not always easy to read the jaw numbers or their corresponding slot numbers.

To overcome the problem I simply colour-coded each mating jaw and slot in highly coloured enamel paints. No 1 I coloured black, No 2 yellow, No 3 red, and No 4 green. They can all be easily identified, even in poor light.

A word of warning, however. All mating and sliding surfaces must be kept clean and free of paint or the chuck may not function smoothly. Paint must only be applied to the outside surfaces of the chuck body and jaws.

Davey Richardson, 8 Heath Rise, Fakenham, Norfolk NR21 8HU.

The same effect can be achieved by using small pieces of coloured sticky tape - Ed.

4   Indexing Ring with a Difference

Has any reader thought of using a lathe-mounted key-operated Jacobs chuck as an indexing ring? I've been using mine for some time, with very accurate results.

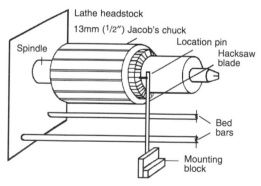

Lathe headstock
13mm (1/2") Jacob's chuck
Location pin
Spindle
Hacksaw blade
Bed bars
Mounting block

The toothed edge of the chuck where the key is normally engaged serves the same purpose as an indexing ring. Location is by a spring-loaded pin screwed to the lathe bed.

A hacksaw blade cut to the required length with the teeth ground off makes a suitable spring. The existing hole in one end of the hacksaw blade is used to take a bolt which is ground to a tight fit in one of the chuck indentations.

Although smaller than the average indexing plate, this device can be used to accurately locate any workpiece for spiral work, fluting, or any other task calling for a variety of dividing operations.

Small diameters can be fitted directly into the chuck and larger diameters accommodated between centres or on a backing plate mounted in the chuck.

My chuck has 30 indentations and a selection of locations are shown in the following table:

No. of positions required	Angle in degrees	Holes used
2	180	1-16
3	120	1-11-21
5	72	1-7-13-19-25
6	60	1-6-11-16-21-26
10	36	1-4-7-10-13-16-19-22-25-28 30
12	All	

N.S. Davies, 10 St Davids Road, Miskin, Pontyclun, Mid Glamorgan.

5 Revolving Centre

I used the parts of a broken flexible drive to make a useful revolving centre. The chuck can hold any number of home-made fittings.

The flexible component was discarded and the solid shaft at the chuck end shortened. The bearing from the drive shaft end was mounted behind the chuck bearing.

Both the bearings were fixed firmly using two-part epoxy resin into a carrier made of beech, turned with a taper to fit into my tailstock.

Bill Howard, Trebilcock Cottage, Ponsmere Road, Perranporth, Cornwall TR6 0BW.

6 Socket Drive

I have found that sockets from square drive socket spanner sets make perfect square drives for small sections of wood when mounted in my Coronet chuck. You can use 12mm (1/2″) or 10mm (3/8″) drive sockets according to the size of the wood to be turned.

The wood stock should be slightly oversize and tapered to fit. And of course you can also use the other, 12-point end of the sockets to take various sizes of wood.

Nigel Breeze, 53 Norbroom Drive, Newport, Shropshire TF10 7TE.

7 Tacked On

I find small items such as box lids can be held on to a shaped wooden backplate with Blu-tack for turning. Also a loose fitting cup chuck will hold most items using Blu-tack better than if using a jam fit with chalk or sandpaper.

The great advantage of the material is that it holds well, yet is easily removed, and does not damage polished surfaces. This

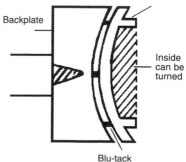

7

means you can finish polish, say, the outside of a box lid and then turn it over and fix it with Blu-tack so you can turn the inside of the lid. Afterwards the lid is just pulled off the backing plate.

PJ. Barnes, Callymoor House, Peter Tavy, Tavistock, Devon PL19 9NN.

8 Wood Chuck Screws

I have a useful method of mounting my home-made wooden chucks to my lathe which ensures they are always centred accurately.

I have simply replaced the woodscrew of my screwchuck with an engineering screw or bolt (I used an M10). I then put threaded inserts of the appropriate size into the wooden chucks. They are thus easily removed and always centred.

I use the same method for mounting my grinding and sharpening device. This is simply a disc turned from three layers of 20mm (3/4") MDF to a diameter that matches the grinding belts for standard bench grinders. I use zirconium corundum belts that are specially made by SIA in Switzerland for grinding HSS tools.

Markus Ellermeier, Briesbach 15, D-55743 Idar-Oberstein, Germany.

SECTION 2   LATHES

1 Easy Measure

Here's a tip for owners of modern Coronet lathes. Several chucks on the market require 38mm (1¹/2") DIA spigots, dovetails or recesses for split rings etc.

If you are using one, simply set your callipers to the round bed bars of the lathe. As Coronet bed bars are 38mm (1¹/2") DIA there is no need to check with a rule.

Gavin Chapman, 21 Caernarvon Avenue, Garforth, Leeds, West Yorkshire LS25 2LQ.

2 Home-made Lathe

Having decided to try my hand at woodturning, but not being able to afford a lathe, I decided - after reading your magazine - to make one. I already owned a power drill.

The base, measuring 915mm x 215mm x 25mm (3' x 8¹/2" x 1"), was given to me, and the revolving vice cost £6.50 from the local market. It holds a length of aluminium 'T' section 10 gauge for

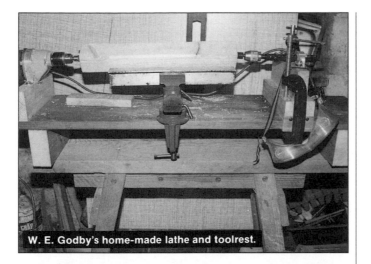

W. E. Godby's home-made lathe and toolrest.

The tailstock set-up.

the toolrest.

The tailstock is made from part of a hand brace, secured with 16 gauge aluminium strips. The wood holding the tailstock had to slide freely with two pieces of aluminium angle 10 gauge to guide it.

Two 'G' cramps bought for £1.00 each in the market do a good job in holding the unit secure. The centres were also cheap market buys.

My lathe has a 125mm (5″) swing and 460mm (18″) between

centres. I found this ended up much cheaper than a lathe attachment costing about £60.

I've yet to make a faceplate from mild steel plate. I'm lucky to have been left three gouges by my father-in-law.

W.E. Godby, 30 Rochester Avenue, Rochester, Kent ME1 2DW.

3 Lathe Refinements

When I bought a Record DML24 lathe I found that the locking/adjustment arrangement for the toolrest, tailstock and belt-changing compartment was by means of three different sized hexagonal socket-head screws. No keys were provided with the kit.

I found this fiddly and decided to customise and improve my lathe. I brazed suitably shortened Allen keys to the screws and turned some nice pear shaped handles for them in ebonite.

The banjo adjustment and tailstock-to-bed clamp were fixed with bolts needing a separate spanner. On to these bolt heads I brazed 6mm ($1/4''$) rods and fitted more turned ebonite handles to these.

The result of these modifications is a more up-market machine that is much slicker to use.

If you are unable to braze on the knobs you could use superglue, or the rods could be welded to the bolts by a local garage.

Further refinements would be to make a tab washer for the banjo adjusting nut and to remove the bolt head locating lands from the bottom of the staps.

Alistair Wales, 22 Barnard Road, Billingham, Cleveland TS23 2HG.

4 Modified Lathe

Some of Mr Davies' work produced on the modified lathe.

More than six months ago I became the proud owner of a Record DML24 lathe, which proved to be ideal for my needs as a beginner, being simple to set up, vibration-free and quiet in operation.

However, having mastered the rudiments of

The modified Record DML24 lathe

the craft, I wanted to progress to turning larger diameter bowls than that allowed by the 230mm (9″) capacity of this machine.

To achieve this without having to buy a more expensive lathe, I resorted to the following:

1. Removed the tailstock and toolpost assembly from the lathe bed.
2. Repositioned the headstock at the tail-end of the bed.
3. Fitted a removable stabilising saddle behind the headstock - fabricated from a piece of 100mm x 50mm (4″x 2″) timber which is secured by a bolt through the lathe bench.
4. Fitted the toolpost assembly at the outboard end of the lathe bench on a prefabricated bracket which is bolted to the bench to the left of the centre line. This allows the toolrest's swing to cover both the face and edge of a larger diameter workpiece. With this arrangement, I can easily turn bowls of 305mm (12″) DIA with a depth of 63mm (2¹/₂″) without any apparent overloading of the lathe motor or excessive vibration.

I have not given details about how to build the outboard toolpost assembly, as I am sure readers wanting to make these modifications will have their own ideas on this.

Note that the above does not involve any changes to the lathe's components, and requires only one hole in the lathe bench to take the saddle bolt.

I should add that I am aged 73 and had no experience of any woodwork before a friend gave me a copy of *Woodturning* about a year ago. My interest in the craft was immediately aroused and I have since become a regular subscriber.

Undaunted by my ignorance and with considerable trial and error and frequent references to *Woodturning* magazine, I now produce some acceptable pieces.

N.S. Davies, 10 St Davids Road, Miskin, Pontyclun, Mid Glamorgan CF7 8PW.

5 Poolewood Lathe Modifications

Following Reg Sherwin's useful article on modifications to his Poolewood lathe (*Woodturning*, Issue 24), I wonder if other Poolewood owners have had the problem I have with the locking levers on the toolrest and would like to use my solution?

These two levers are continually working loose without my noticing and, I believe, as a result snapped at the beginning of the thread within a week of each other.

My local DIY shop stocks a hanger bolt or wood/metal screw which is available in lengths from 38mm - 76mm (1^1/2-3"). It has an ordinary wood screw at one end and 10mm (^{3}/8") Whitworth thread at the other. There are also 50mm (2") screws with M6 thread.

Pop a locking nut on, screw it into the toolpost locking ring as far as you can without binding on the post, lock it up, turn a new handle for it, drill out a hole for the woodscrew end and wind it on - job done.

Well, not quite, as I found the screw is mild steel and bends a bit. When I find time I'm going to harden it. My engineering friend tells me I need oil to temper the screw, as quenching in water will make it too brittle.

It cost me about 30p - and it doesn't come undone.

Peter Hoole, Little Grove House, Cumberland Gardens, Tunbridge Wells, Kent TN1 1UQ.

Stick tape over bolt slot

6 Sealed Bolt Slot

I have solved the problem of my toolrest becoming stiff and difficult to adjust because of a build-up of chips and shavings in the banjo bolt slot.

I first cleaned the assembly, and then stuck a strip of adhesive carpet tape 215mm x 50mm (8^1/2" x 2") wide over the bolt slot, with a small kink in the tape lengthwise to clear the end of the bolt.

The result is a nice smooth toolrest slide, as the slot is sealed and dust free.

I use a Coronet No 1, but I'm sure other lathes have a similar toolrest problem curable by this method.

Richard Pain, 88 Windermere Avenue, Ramsgate, Kent CT11 0PL.

TOOLS SECTION 3

1 Belt Sander Sharpening Jig

I have made a special guide for my belt sander (see Photo 1) which ensures accuracy when sharpening bowl turning gouges.

I bolted an angle iron from my local hardware store to the belt sander's guide, using a coach bolt and a wing nut. The angle iron should be strong and it pays to take a square to the shop to check the angle.

I fixed a piece of sandpaper with double-sided tape to the angle iron, so increasing friction between it and the belt sander's guide, enabling the iron to stay in place more readily.

1. Belt sander with angle iron bolted on

The wide iron angle I use is particularly suitable for sharpening long, bowl turning gouges. For small, carving gouges a smaller iron is needed.

2. Plywood backing plate

This set-up allows you to grind an even bevel at any chosen angle and gives a superb edge. It is a quick and easy method and also saves blade length.

The only drawback, particularly for amateurs working evenings and weekends, is the noise of the belt sander. I decided to buy an ELU MWA 149 (Photos 2 and 3), as described in Issue 17 of *Woodturning*.

I bolted a piece of plywood to the linisher's housing and an angle iron to the plywood, as already described. If you can work aluminium this might be better than plywood.

3. Correct tool bevel achieved

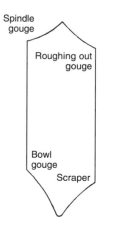

A simple indexing device can be added easily. I drilled a 2mm (³/32″) hole into the angle iron near the upper corner.

Then I used cardboard templates to set the angle iron to different angles (35, 45 and 60 DEG). For each position I drilled a hole into the plywood, using the 2mm (³/32″) hole in the angle iron as a guide.

A nail (with its point removed for safety) inserted through both holes completes the indexing device. The upper corner of the angle iron can be used as a pointer when you write the different angles onto the plywood.

I use the supported part of the belt for sanding, as otherwise the bevel becomes convex. For small angles you need to move the angle iron to the right (towards the big wheel).

Kai Kothe, Klosterberg 3, 65779 Kelkheim, Germany.

2 Grinding Template

Much time can be wasted at the grinding wheel trying to produce a single bevel. The experts make it look easy, but most of us are not experts.

The turning tool can easily be held steady if it is laid flat on the platform rest of the grinder. The only problem then is the accurate setting of the platform angle.

I made a template of the platform and grinding wheel edge for the various tool angles. The material is clear plastic, and the construction took about ten minutes.

First decide on the tool angle and set the platform accordingly. Put one straight edge of the plastic on the platform and grind a curve with the wheel. Use different sides for different angles.

Once made the template is a joy to use as the correct angle can be set instantly, and the tool ground in seconds, with a nice clean single bevel.

Dr Michael Culloty, 85 Rowlands Avenue, Pinner, Middlesex HA5 4AW.

3 Burning Tool

I have tried holding a piece of wire against turning work such as boxes or tool handles to create decorative lines. At first I held the wire in my hands, but after burning my fingers several times I thought there must be a better way. You can hold the ends of the wire with pliers, but that is awkward.

In the end I made a plywood frame, shaped a bit like a hacksaw or fretsaw, and fastened the wire using 5mm x 55mm (³/16″ x 2¹/4″) eye bolts and nuts. The eyes are countersunk

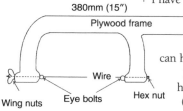

380mm (15″)
Plywood frame
Wire
Wing nuts   Eye bolts   Hex nut

into the frame so they don't turn when being tightened. A 15mm (⁵/₈″) thick plywood frame works better than metal as it does not vibrate so much.

It works well. You must first mark a groove on the turning work with the sharp or long point of a skew so the wire doesn't wander. The secret of good burning is a nice tight wire. You just hold the wire in place until you see smoke or until you get a nice colour.

Harold Miller, 230 Pleasantview Drive, Hamilton, Illinois 62341, USA.

4 Calliper Scale

The tip for a double-ended calliper in Issue 16 of *Woodturning* offers little advantage over the usual type of calliper, unless the lip of the vessel is thicker than the wall being measured.

In this case the gap is measured at one end of the calliper while the other end is in contact with the wall. This requires juggling with a ruler.

It helps to make a scale at one end for direct reading. The scale may be made more sensitive by increasing the length of the calliper leg on that side.

John G. Taylor, 420 Leymoor Road, Golcar, Huddersfield, West Yorkshire HD7 4QF.

5 Circular Glass Cutter

As a woodturner and picture framer, I am often asked to turn circular frames of varying sizes for mirrors and pieces of embroidery etc.

While the making and turning of frames presents few problems, the cutting of the glass and mirrors to fit can be difficult.

Having tried freehand and round templates, I looked into buying a commercially made cutter, but this was too expensive.

The answer was to make my own circular glass cutter (FIG 1), and this has proved to be a great success.

The method is to score a circle using a trammel, then score lines radially from the circle outwards (FIG 2). Tap and then break away the outer pieces.

Paul Nicholson, The Joiners Shop, Blacktoft, Yorkshire DN14 7YW.

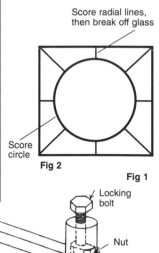

Score radial lines, then break off glass

Score circle

Fig 2

Fig 1

Slot

Hole

Clamp bolt

Glass cutter

Locking bolt

Nut

Turned barrel

Pivot

Clearance holes

Rubber sucker of toy arrow

15

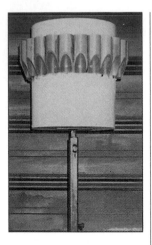

6   Drum Chisel Stand

I made this circular chisel stand from pieces of plastic tubing glued and rivetted to a drum, which is itself attached to an adjustable metal stand.

The plastic tubes which hold the chisels are 100mm long x 25mm (4" x 1") DIA, cut obliquely at 45 DEG at the base. They are glued on to the 305mm long x 250mm (12" x 9³/4") DIA drum with blue PVC cement, and one pop rivet near the base of each tube.

The stand is made of an inner and outer tube. The outer tube is 850mm long (33³/8") with an inside diameter of 18mm (²³/32"). Inside this fits the inner tube which is 500mm long x 16mm (19¹/2" x ²¹/32") DIA. A 10mm (³/8") nut with bolt is welded on to the outer tube so the stand can be adjusted for height.

On top of the inner tube is welded a 100mm square x 3mm (4"x ¹/8") thick metal plate. On to this is welded a 180mm x 12mm (7" x ¹/2") rod.

Two 12mm (¹/2") thick circular boards are cut to fit inside the drum, one at the base and the other half way up. These are fixed with glue and self-tapping screws. Central holes are drilled in the boards to take bushes which hold the rod, so the drum can be turned round.

The stand is welded to a 500mm (19⁵/8") plough disc which makes a secure base.

John Brooks, 97 Whitfield Street, Bassendean, WA 6054, USA.

7   Dual-purpose Spanner

Lathe spanner size

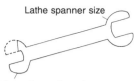

Ground scraping edge

I modified my combination spanner on the angle grinder, making one end the right size for adjusting my lathe, and the other a scraper for working over-hanging bowls with narrow openings.

James Edgar, Left Hand Turning, Pullens Cottage, Lower Eggleton, Nr Ledbury, Herefordshire HR8 2UJ.

8   Dust Extractor Funnel

A metal funnel with a flexible metal hose of the kind used by garages for pouring oil into car engines makes a good dust extractor nozzle.

It can easily be bent into a suitable position or moved out of the way (Photos 1 and 2). An adaptor for the hose of your shop vacuum might be needed.

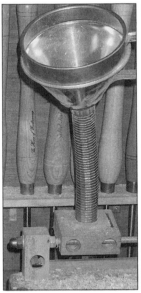

My funnel moves along a threaded rod fixed to a wooden board bolted to the lathe bed. A weight is used to counterbalance the weight of the funnel (Photo 3).

Clamps hold the threaded rod in position and allow easy removal in case the setup gets in the way. The funnel could, of course, be used with an independent stand or be fixed to the wall.

Kai Kothe, Klosterberg 3, 65779 Kelkheim, Germany.

1. Funnel with flexible hose mounted on the lathe bed

2. Funnel can be moved to any suitable position

3. A spanner used as a counterbalance weight

9 Easy Bandsaw Blade Changing

A few months ago I bought an Elu/DeWalt 3401 bandsaw. While finding it a good machine, I had difficulty changing blades because of the small gap through which they have to be inserted in the guard and then turned.

The answer, I decided, was to make the front of the guard hinged. The first step was to drill a 9mm ($^{11}/_{32}$″) hole 28mm ($1^{1}/_{8}$″) in from the side panel and 150mm (6″) down from the top, at the rear of the bandsaw.

I removed the blade, then unscrewed and removed the guard

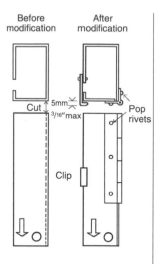

Before modification   After modification

Cut 5mm
3/16" max

Pop rivets

Clip

section. I put the guard in a vice and cut off the front with a hacksaw as close to the bend as possible. The rough edges were cleaned up with a file.

I then fitted a 130mm (5¹/8″) length of piano hinge, with the hinge pin outermost, using pop rivets. A small metal or plastic clip was fitted as shown to complete the job.

By opening the front of the guard it is now easy to change blades, and the protection is still 100% as the front will only open when the plastic bandsaw cover is removed and the safety switch is off.

P.B. Sawyer, 34 Merynton Avenue, Coventry CV4 7BN.

10 Gutter Toolrack

To keep my tools tidy, I fastened a length of rainwater guttering to the wall above my lathe with brackets. It was left over from my shed, so cost me nothing.

Now I can see all my tools clearly without having to search among the shavings, and there is no chance of grabbing the wrong end.

Another tip is to use a piece of twinwall left over from roofing for storing pencils or ballpoint pens. Simply clip it into a spare end piece of aluminium or plug it with a grooved piece of wood which can be screwed to the wall.

R. Flint, 2 Marshall Court, Balderton, Newark, Nottinghamshire NG24 3NL.

11 Lathe Tool Tidy

This tool tidy was chiefly designed for twin-bed Record/Coronet lathes (0-3 series), but with a little modification it can be made to suit almost any twin-bedded lathe, and possibly some square sectioned single-bed lathes as well.

It takes less than half an hour to make, including marking and cutting out time. The finished tool tidy prevents the four or five chisels you may be using while working on the lathe from rolling about and keeps them handy, safe and visible.

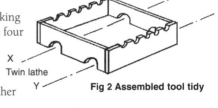

X

Twin lathe

Y

Fig 2 Assembled tool tidy

Another advantage is that the tool tidy can be used either side of the tailstock, depending on whether you are spindle or bowl turning. It can also be easily moved and placed on any flat surface.

Using a 12mm (1/2″) thick piece of plywood, or something similar, measuring 510mm x 100mm (20″x 4″), mark out as shown in FIG 1. Dimensions x and y are the centrepoint of each of the lathe-bed bars.

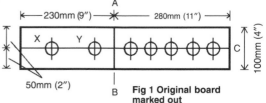

Fig 1 Original board marked out

Therefore, for the Record/Coronet lathe, drill the two holes 38mm (1¹/2″) DIA, some 100mm (4″) apart, using a hole cutting saw from both sides. These holes would be square for a Tyme Avon lathe and would be sawn after cutting along line C-D.

The five holes which form the recesses for the chisels, are drilled 20mm (3/4″) DIA, again using the hole saw. These holes can be equally spaced, but this is mainly determined by the size of your chisel handles.

Saw along lines A,B,C and D, smoothing the edges and face to your usual standard. Construct as in FIG 2, using PVA wood glue and 20mm (3/4″) panel pins. Allow 24 hours to dry before using.

R.M. Parry, 14 Chiltern Close, Oakham, Leicester LE15 6NW.

12 Log Holding Jig

I have invented a jig which safely holds a log for cutting with a chainsaw, as both hands remain free to operate and control the saw.

It can take all log sizes, simply by adjusting the height of the holding bar. The log can also be swivelled on the pointed holding down pin.

The holding chain at the top keeps the pressure arm down and secure.

The jig is made from 25mm (1″) galvanised pipe, which I find quite strong for holding large logs. I made the fourth leg adjustable so as to level.

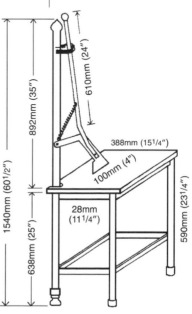

The base board is five-ply, and on top of this I put a piece of deal for the saw to cut into, sparing the base board.

The frame can be made any size, but I find the size shown in the drawing to be the most convenient for storage and transport.

Best of all, the jig will save accidents such as cut legs etc., and one person can easily cut a log.

As a pensioner who has had several tussles with logs in his time, I value this jig and hope it will benefit others who have a fight during their wood preparation.

R.D. McKay, 5 Lima Street, Gosnells 6110, Western Australia.

13 Log Saw Horse

Cheap, small 255mm (10") chain saws are handy when you do not have a big capacity bandsaw for cutting billets into fairly round balanced bowl blanks - but you have to be careful.

This improvised safety support, clamped to the bench or laid on the ground, will hold a half section log very steady while you cut. It also avoids the saw blade blunting as it would if you cut through the log carelessly and touched the ground.

Provide extra holes so the dowels can be moved to suit different sizes and shapes.

Extra sockets

Moveable 20mm x 140mm long dowel (3/4" x 51/2").

405mm (16")

200mm (8") 25mm (1")

Softwood or MDF base

Saw horse for bowl blank trimming

Bill Kinsman, 9 Vanity Close, Oulton, Stone, Staffordshire ST15 8TZ.

14 Miniature Tools from Flat-bits

I occasionally need miniature turning tools and have found two reasonable sources of steel which can be quickly ground to the required shape.

From my local surplus store I bought an 8mm flat-bit to which I attached a handle, then ground off the points on either side and modified the angle of the main point to produce a 1.5mm wide mini-parting tool.

Care is needed to avoid overheating the fine tip, both when grinding and in use, and more aggressive grinding may be necessary later to remove holes or deeply impressed size markings which many of these bits contain.

It won't last as long as a Superflute, but for £1.69 and the time to turn a handle, I'm not moaning.

These small flat-bits can also be ground to form light-duty

miniature scrapers or skews, having the advantage of a fairly long shaft.

But for something sturdier, and even cheaper, I bought a couple of 3/8″ cold-chisels for 34p each, fitted them into 255mm (10″) handles with about 63mm (2¹/2″) of their 106mm (4¹/4″) length projecting, and ground square and round scrapers on the ends.

Bill Gilson, 7 Addington Road, Trimley St. Mary, Suffolk IP10 0UQ.

15 Offset Lathe Tools from Bolts

For those who need small, offset lathe tools, the easiest and cheapest thing in the USA to make them out of is Grade 8 bolts.

These are the high carbon bolts in the 4140 series of steel, used for lorries and other heavy equipment. They are available in many sizes, from 6mm (¹/4″) to 38mm (1¹/2″) DIA and up to 255mm (10″) long.

First heat to bend · Second heat to draw temper

First determine how long the tool needs to be. Then grind off the head of the bolt or cut to the desired length. The threaded end will be used later.

With a propane torch or stove flame heat the area to be bent until it is red hot, bend it in a vice or with pliers, then quench in an oil bath or with an air blast from a compressor. The latter is preferred, because it is easier on the steel.

Now grind the tip to the profile wanted, leaving it rather heavy, not a final grind. Make sure the top of the cutting edge has a bright shine to it for the next step.

Take the torch and gently heat just behind the cutting edge until the polished steel turns to the colour of straw. This is called drawing the temper. Quench again and make the final grind.

Now turn a handle and bore a hole in it slightly smaller than the bolt's diameter. Using the thread on the end of the bolt, screw the shank of the newly-made tool into the handle - and there you have it.

It may sound complex, but the whole exercise (including turning the handle) shouldn't take more than 10 minutes. You also have the option of forging a particular shape at the business end of the tool in the first heating if you have a small anvil.

Buz Blum, Box 732, Palmer, Alaska 99645, USA.

Grade 8 bolts are equivalent to high tensile bolts in the UK - Ed.

16 Scrapers & Skews from Spanners

Old files can make excellent turning tools, but there is always the danger of the brittle metal fracturing or, worse still, shattering, with disastrous results. And not all of us have the skills to re-temper files.

To overcome this, yet still make your own oval skew chisels and shaped scrapers, old chrome vanadium spanners - commonly found in car boot sales or street markets - can be used.

Most ring spanners have oval shafts perfectly shaped for converting to skew chisels, while the shafts of open ended spanners are usually flat and so more suitable for turning into shaped scrapers.

To convert these tools is quite simple. It involves grinding or cutting off the ends of the spanners, grinding one end to shape, and forming a tang on the other to fit your turned handle.

Chrome vanadium is easily ground and honed to razor sharpness and in practice has proved nearly as durable as HSS. The only difference is the price.

A set of three skews and three assorted shaped scrapers cost me the princely sum of £1.50 - for the spanners, as the ferrules came from scrap brass piping and the handles from ash offcuts.

N.S. Davies, 10 St Davids Road, Miskin, Pontyclun, Mid Glamorgan.

17 Small Power Sanding

For months I thought about ways of cutting down sanding time on my woodturning. Using a sanding disc in a power drill works well on large areas, but something smaller is needed for delicate work.

I have found the answer to be a Black & Decker power file. This has a straight arm for flat surfaces, and a cranked arm for curved surfaces. They take 6mm (1/4") and 13mm (1/2") wide abrasive belts.

If you use the file going against the direction of the lathe it gives a coarse sanding or cutting action, while if you use the file going in the same direction as the lathe it gives a good polishing or smoothing action.

I find this tool works on both soft and hard woods and saves much sanding time on spindles, hollow vessels, bowls and round discs for plates and clocks.

S. Ashworth, 1 Richmond Close, Tottington, Bury, Lancs.

18 Tight Fitting Ferrules

When turning your own tool handles and fitting brass ferrules,

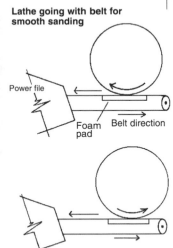

Lathe going with belt for smooth sanding

Power file

Foam pad — Belt direction

Lathe going against belt for coarse sanding

make the diameter of the spigot slightly larger than the internal diameter of the ferrule.

Put the ferrule in an old pan or metal container, pour in boiling water, and leave to simmer for a few minutes before removing with pliers.

The heat will cause the ferrule to expand and it will slide easily over the spigot. When it cools it will fit tightly and there is no chance of it coming off.

Gavin Chapman, 21 Caernarvon Avenue, Garforth, Leeds, West Yorkshire LS25 2LQ.

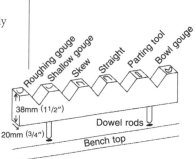

19 Turning Tool Sorter

To avoid constantly hunting for my turning tools covered in shavings beneath the lathe, I devised and made this sorter rack which fits on the bench top under the lathe bed bars.

Each cut out V holds a separate tool, and a symbol is marked beside it for easy identification. Of course any number of positions can be made, and the rack can be any length required.

The rack is made from 38mm x 20mm (1¹/2"x ³/4") wood and is fitted to the bench top by means of two dowel rods which slot into pre-drilled holes. Two or three sets of holes can be drilled to place the rack in a number of positions.

The rack can be easily removed so the bench can be swept. The bench can thus be kept tidy and safe, with no tools rolling around or falling on the floor.

D. Gledhill, 12 South View, Scapegoat Hill, Huddersfield, W. Yorks HD7 4NU.

20 What Price HSS Tools?

I looked with envy at HSS gouges and decided to make my own. First I found an old HSS thread cutting tap at a car boot sale, measuring 200mm long x 12mm (8"x ¹/2") thick.

You cannot cut this stuff with a hacksaw, so I ground a groove around the shaft and broke off the cutting part in the vice.

Using a 38mm x 6mm (1¹/2" x ¹/4") grindstone for use in an electric drill, I set it up to form a temporary flute grinder, as shown in the drawing. It's a safe system and easier to use than a grindstone. A fence or guide can be fixed to the table if required.

Round carbon or HSS steel can also be bought and used, creating

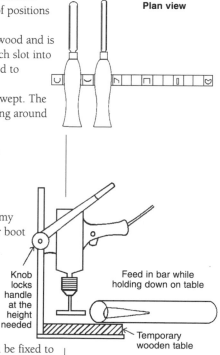

considerable savings and giving you the satisfaction of having made your own gouges.

L.J. Jackson, 28 Nant Hall Road, Prestatyn, Clwyd LL19 9LN.

Eye protection should be worn for all grinding operations, of course - Ed.

SECTION 4   TURNING TECHNIQUES

1 Bowl Blank Guide

A useful guide for marking out planks before cutting bowl blanks can be made from plywood discs of various diameters fitted with a block of wood for a handgrip. At dead centre a nail protrudes by about 3mm (^{1}/8″).

Fit the chosen disc (6mm (^{1}/4″) thick) to the plank by tapping with a hammer, and run a pencil around the circumference for an accurately marked blank.

Burrs and natural-edged blanks are cut by extending the centre nail to 12mm (^{1}/2″) or longer, depending on the roughness of the half log to be cut.

After a good whack with the hammer to seat the disc, the blank is run through the bandsaw, keeping the blade just clear of the edge of the disc.

One word of warning: unless you keep the disc clear of the blade, the unsupported edges can flip up if contacted.

These plywood guides offer a quick way of getting near perfect blanks with little fiddling about.

Ron Fernie, Abernethy Woodturning, Glenfoot, Abernethy, Perthshire PH2 9LS.

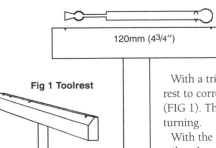

120mm (4³/4″)

Fig 1 Toolrest

2 By the Mark

The following two tips for marking tool rests and tailstocks have helped me a lot since I became a full time woodturner two years ago.

With a triangular file I cut grooves in a blacksmith's-made tool rest to correspond with the required dimensions of a lace bobbin (FIG 1). This removes the need to mark up each blank when turning.

With the same file I cut grooves 10mm (^{3}/8″) apart on my tailstock to show how deep a drill hole goes when the tailstock is wound in (FIG 2). I have been buying your excellent magazine since Issue No. 1. Keep up the good work and long may woodturners share their ideas with each other.

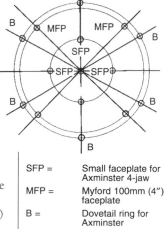

Fig 2 Tailstock

James Edgar, Left Hand Turning, Pullens Cottage, Lower Eggleton, Nr Ledbury, Herefordshire HR8 2UJ.

3 Centring Jigs

I have made some centring jigs from 3mm (¹/8″) thick clear plastic to save wood and speed up my lathe fixings.

The larger jig is 460mm (18″) square with concentric circles scribed at 12mm (¹/2″) spacings.

The circles were scribed with a point on a trammel bar, and the grooves filled with different coloured poster paints (black, red and yellow) to make them easy to read on all types of wood.

The smaller jigs are 125mm (5″) square and were made to suit my chucking systems (Multistar and Myford/Axminster), but could be adapted to other systems.

In the centre of the small jigs I have fixed a small self tapping screw with the end ground to a point.

In use, the large jig is placed over the wood blank and the centre marked with a bradawl. The small jig is then centred on this mark and the fixing points for the chosen ring or faceplate marked. The blank is then ready for drilling and fixing.

Michael Stratton, 1 Meon Road, Mickleton, Chipping Campden, Glos. GL55 6TB.

4 Clamp Conversion

Not everyone has a bandsaw for trimming large blocks of wood to rough size for bowl blanks before turning. I trim blanks on a bench or Workmate using a hand or power saw, and I have come up with this useful clamp conversion to hold them steady while cutting.

This converts a normal 150mm x 75mm (6″ x 3″) clamp into a deep throat 255mm (10″) clamp.

You will need two pieces of 38mm x 38mm (1¹/2″ x 1¹/2″) angle iron 255mm (10″) long. This is about 5mm (³/16″) thick. You will also need four 50mm (2″) long pieces of 25mm x 6mm (1″ x ¹/4″) flat iron.

Jig for Multistar chuck

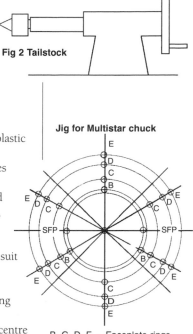

B C D E = Faceplate rings
SFP = Small faceplate

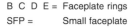

Jig for Myford/Axminster chucks

SFP =	Small faceplate for Axminster 4-jaw
MFP =	Myford 100mm (4″) faceplate
B =	Dovetail ring for Axminster

25

Grind the back web of the clamp to make sure it is flat smooth. Drill four 10mm 3/8" DIA holes in the clamp, one opposite the top jaw and the others at 25mm 1" intervals down the middle of the back web.

Weld two of the pieces of flat iron inside each of the angle iron sections. Drill a 10mm 3/8" hole 15mm 5/8" from the end of the flat iron pieces and bolt them to the clamp frame with 38mm 1 1/2" bolts.

A.R. Taylor, The Hollies, Whitwell Road, Sparham, Norwich, Norfolk NR9 5PW.

5 Clean Bottoms

Most turners nowadays like to remove all traces of chucking methods from the bottom of their bowls, whether they be footed or recessed.

The traditional way is to insert the rim of the bowl into a jam chuck, but a new chuck has to be made for every different size of bowl.

Modern combination chucks can be fitted with wooden jaws and the bowl rim held in expansion mode, but the amount of jaw movement is only about 6mm (1/4"), so you cannot accommodate a large range of bowl sizes with just one set.

My method, although not so accurate, will accept bowls of any size, the largest limited only by the size of swing over the lathe bed. First cut a large disc of 18mm (3/4") or 25mm (1") thick MDF, mount it on the faceplate and true it up. Then stick a piece of sheet rubber (such as an old car tyre inner tube) flat onto the face.

Spin the disc on the lathe and mark a series of circles on the rubber, or score with the point of a skew.

The other component is a hardwood cone made to fit snugly over a revolving tailstock centre. On the end of the cone (about 12mm (1/2") DIA) glue a rubber washer.

After turning the outside of a bowl, giving it either a recess or a

Faceplate
Rubber covered disk
Bowl
Cone with rubber washer
Clean up outside of foot or remove recess
Tailstock

foot to be held in the chuck, I finish sand and polish the inside of the recess or bottom of the foot. I then mount the bowl on the chuck and complete the inside of the bowl.

I replace the chuck with the rubber-covered disc and place the bowl rim onto the disc, using the circles to centre it as near as possible.

I bring up the tailstock and cone to hold the bowl firmly. I can then clean up the edge of the foot, removing any chuck marks, or turn off the recess completely. The bottom can then be sanded and finished by blending in the polish.

Peter Symonds, Doublesse House, The Drift, Exning, Newmarket, Suffolk CB8 7EZ.

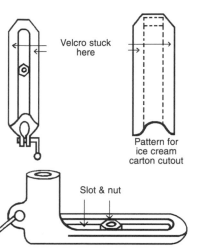

Velcro stuck here

Pattern for ice cream carton cutout

Slot & nut

6 Cutting Clogging

Here's a cheap and easy way to overcome the problem of a banjo toolrest slot clogging with chips and dust or, worse still, dried sap after turning green wood.

First you will need the top of an ice cream carton (the flexible plastic type about 1.5mm ($^1/16''$) thick which is easy to cut with a knife or scissors).

Next, a packet of Velcro Stick n' Stick strip, measuring 20mm x 45mm ($^3/4''$ x 1$^3/4''$) and costing about 95p.

Cut two Velcro strips long enough to run the length of both sides of the banjo slot, out of the hook half of the strip. The leftover piece will fill in the gap at the end of the slot.

Next, cut the ice cream top into a strip wide enough to cover the slot and the stuck-on strips of Velcro.

I also fitted the plastic around the base of the toolrest post, to seal the slot completely.

All that remains is to stick the corresponding Velcro strip to the underside of this for a good seal. The slight give in the Velcro allows the nut to slide up and down the slot with no tightening but, should the need arise to remove the whole toolrest assembly, you can just pull off this top seal.

Robert Smith, 7 Holmlea Road, Goring-on-Thames, Nr Reading, Berkshire RG8 9EX.

7 Marking Blanks before Bandsawing

Here is a useful tip for marking a circle on the rough side of a piece of wood before bandsawing for a turning blank. I've often done this on half a log (FIG 1).

Fig 1 Drilling the Log

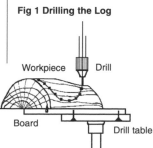

Workpiece   Drill

Board

Drill table

I use a standard pillar drill press with rotating table and you will also need a piece of 20mm (3/4″) blockboard about 405mm x 230mm (16″ x 9″).

In the centre of this, and 150mm (6″) from one end, a woodscrew is inserted, with the head sawn off so the shank protrudes about 12mm (1/2″) above the surface.

The sawn-off end of the screw is rounded with a file.

The board is then fastened onto the drill table so that the table's centre is about 115mm (41/2″) in from the end of the board (the opposite end from the screw).

This is done by screwing from underneath the table to leave a flush top on the board.

Using compasses, the required circle is marked on the flat side of the workpiece and a 15mm (5/8″) deep hole is drilled at the centre, with a diameter to fit over the cut-off screw on the board.

A small drill (say 3mm (1/8″)) is placed in the chuck and the table height adjusted to accommodate the workpiece, making use of the full depth of feed.

The horizontal position is adjusted so that the distance between the cut-off screw and the drill is equal to the radius required on the workpiece.

Lock the table, locate the workpiece on the cut-off screw on the board and, by rotating the workpiece, drill shallow holes about 12mm (1/2″) apart around the circumference (FIG 2).

Join these holes with a felt tip pen and you then have a cutting line for bandsawing. You could even put the pen in the drill chuck and mark similar positions with the drill switched off.

The dimensions given are those I use, but can of course be varied to suit the drill press used.

E. Donald Taylor, 172 Buckstones Road, Shaw, Oldham, Lancashire OL2 8DN.

Fig 2 Plan view of drill table

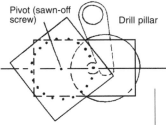

Pivot (sawn-off screw)   Drill pillar

8 Sizing Spigots Easily

People who have trouble with loose fitting spindles should find the following tip useful.

When I need a spigot on the end of a leg or spindle, to fit into a pre-drilled hole, I first measure the spindle's correct length with it on my Coronet lathe, including the length of the tenon.

I then hold an open-ended spanner over the spindle with one hand and cut the wood to the spanner's size with a parting tool held in the other.

When the spanner just fits over the tenon it is the correct size to fit the pre-drilled hole. A half-inch spanner, for example, sizes a half-inch tenon, to fit a half-inch hole.

R.A. Peterson, Westview Cottage, West End, Stainforth, Doncaster, South Yorkshire DN7 5SA.

9 Sphere-Turning Jig

I find using a 4mm (^{5}/32″) O ring in my jig/steady for turning spheres gives a better drive, and less pressure has to be applied to the tailstock.

I made two, one as in the drawing the other a push fit on the running centre. The O rings can be bought at any builders' merchants. Mine were made from a 32mm (1^1/4″) waste pipe elbow and cost 40p.

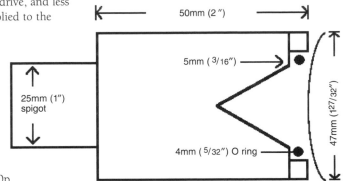

R.H. Garratt, Lynton, 31 Ryland Road, Welton, Lincoln LN2 3LU.

10 Three of the Best

Readers may find the following three tips useful. The first is, never throw away old loudspeakers. Fix one at a handy site close to the lathe and its powerful magnet will keep any gouge out of the shavings and to hand.

The second is, when turning wooden fruit a convincing blossom end can be made from gluing a large clove after drilling the appropriate end. The cloves are available from any Asian grocer.

Being an amateur photographer as well as a woodturner, I often have a lot of 35mm film cases that seem too good to throw out. I burn their bottoms with something like a soldering iron (which leaves a hole stronger than one cut with a knife) and use them as internal reservoirs for salt cellars I have turned, after suitably gluing or pinning in.

T. Boxcer, 1 Railway Cottages, Church Road, Ramsden Bellhouse, Billericay, Essex CM11 1PL.

1 Finishing Jig

With oil finishes requiring three or four coats, and needing at least eight hours between coats, it is a problem to support the work while this is going on, and to oil both sides at the same time.

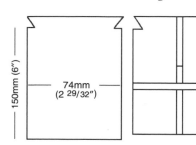

To overcome this, I have devised the following jig, which works well.

I have a Multistar chuck and use it in the expansion mode. The diameter of the hole is 73mm (2⁷/₈"), tapering to 76mm (3¹/₁₆") and 8mm (⁵/₁₆") deep.

I turn a cheap piece of wood (pine or an offcut) to a diameter of 74mm (2²⁹/₃₂") and then form the end as shown, duplicating the shape of the chuck.

I then cut the piece in half longways and glue a piece of wood 4mm (⁵/₃₂") wide to one side on the bottom half only. An elastic band is put round the bottom half to hold them together. To fit to the work, just press the top, place into the work and release.

The jig is easy to make and means you can have more than one piece of work oiled at the same time.

Alan Simmons, 83 West Drive, Cleveleys, Lancashire FY5 2JE.

2 Fluff to Buff

Probably the most satisfying operation on the lathe is the final polishing of your completed project. Unfortunately, it can also be one of the most dangerous.

Cloths and old pieces of rag can easily become caught, with dire consequences.

I found the solution to this in the back of our tumble dryer. The fluff that collects in the filter makes an excellent polishing and buffing cloth. And if by chance it gets caught in a chuck or workpiece it just falls apart.

Best of all, it is extremely cheap.

John Blight, 29 Parkway, Edgcumbe Park, Crowthorne, Berkshire RG11 6EP.

3 Sanding Inside Vessels

I recently had to sand the inside of a deep, narrow-necked vessel and tried the following idea with great success.

Drill a 6mm (¹/₄") hole in a piece of 15mm (⁵/₈") square timber,

Figure labels: 150mm (6"), 74mm (2 29/32")

some 255mm (10″) long and insert the shaft of a Velcro sanding disc (50mm (2″) or smaller) into it. Spin the lathe at 1400 RPM and use the device to sand the vessel's inside.

By using the various grades available, a reasonable finish can be obtained - wherever you can get your hands.

P.B. Sawyer, 34 Merynton Avenue, Coventry CV4 7BN.

4 Sanding Tips

I used to keep my old sandpaper in a plastic bag and had to fish for the right grit whenever I wanted to sand a bowl.

This was time-consuming, so I built a simple sandpaper rack to store the different grits separately, later adding some plastic boxes for Velcro-backed sanding discs (Photo 1).

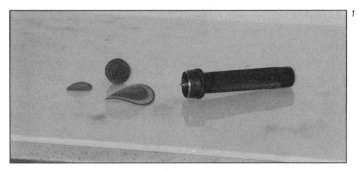

A hollow punch is used to punch out smaller discs

A pair of scissors is kept on the left side of the rack (which also serves as a shelf for my radio).

My second idea concerns making better use of Velcro sanding discs. In bowl sanding (especially the inside) only the outer part of the sanding disc is used, while the middle stays sharp.

You can either keep these discs for sanding jobs where you can use the middle as well, or you can use a hollow punch to punch out a smaller disc for use on a smaller sanding pad (Photo 2).

Kai Kothe, Klosterberg 3, 65779 Kelkheim, Germany.

5 Velcro Disc Blues

If heat generated in my 51mm (2″) foam pad disc-sander is a result of over-aggressive attacks on patches of wild grain, then Murphy's law is at work when, as a result, the Velcro disc detaches itself and inevitably comes to rest, sticky side down in the shavings.

To effect a quick repair, brush off the worst of the shavings and dust from the sticky back, having first removed the sanding disc.

Tip a little cellulose thinner onto a clean rag and wipe the face of the foam pad. Then, without adding more to the rag, lightly rub the reverse of the Velcro which will reactivate the adhesive.

Watch out for Murphy again when bringing the two parts

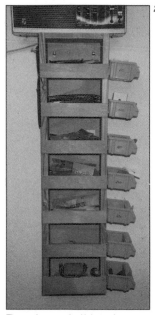

The sandpaper rack with boxes for velcro-backed discs

together, taking care not to touch the prepared surfaces.

While the adhesive is drying, hone up the tool that lifted the grain, something which all Irish woodturners will delight in telling me I should have done in the first place. I hope that gets me off the hook for mentioning Murphy.

Bill Gilson, 7 Addington Road, Trimley St. Mary, Suffolk IP10 0UQ.

6 Wax Melting Pot

I have found a safe way of melting paraffin wax. It came about when the basket on my wife's fat fryer was damaged and I had to buy her a new one.

The old fryer was undamaged apart from the basket, so I put it in my workshop. A few days later I had to seal some blanks and some part-turned bowls to prevent them from splitting.

I had lit my burner and placed my pan of paraffin wax on it when it suddenly came to me: why not use the old fat fryer to melt the wax?

I did this, and found it so much safer than having a naked flame in the workshop. The wax's melting point is about 45 DEG C and the best temperature for sealing I have found to be 120 DEG C. This is about half way between min and max on my fryer gauge setting.

Barry Towell, 15 Wood Road, Kingscliffe, Peterborough, Lincolnshire PE8 6XF.

PART 2

Woodcarving Tips

1 Carving an Otter

Carving an otter and wanting to mount it on a log, I was faced in some degree with a similar problem of getting a snug fit as Ray Gonzales had with the cape on his 'Apparition', described in the first issue of *Woodcarving*.

I thought it would be difficult to clean chalk from the log and I wanted to leave it in its natural state, finished with sanding sealer. Engineers' blue came to mind but that would have made an even bigger mess. Thinking of blue I thought of carbon paper.

I draped a piece of carbon paper over the log, carbon upwards, then placed the roughed out carving over the top. By tapping the carving gently with a mallet it showed up the high spots which were then removed. By repeating this process over and over the required close fit was achieved. (The carbon paper must be for handwriting as typewriter paper is too hard.)

It is important to have some means of location so the carving fits in exactly the same location each time it is replaced.

On my carving this was achieved by using a small cut-off branch on the log as a dowel and boring a suitable hole in the underside of the carving. The second location point was where the feet fitted onto another short branch. Similar location points could be made by using two dowels, or even two thick wood screws with their heads cut off.

I hope this tip will be of assistance to fellow carvers.

Joe Jenkinson, Huddersfield , England.

2 Copy Carving?

I read 'Pointing the way' by Joe Dampf, in the Winter '93 issue with interest. While I do use this technique, particularly when replacing small areas in restoration work, I also use other techniques, especially while creating complete carvings. The first I find much faster than the Joe Dampf method.

Take two sheets of plywood, each larger than the desired carving. Place one on top of the other and mark out with a 25mm (1″) grid. Using a pillar drill, if necessary placed on top of the plywood, drill through both sheets with a 12mm (1/2″) bit on every intersection of the lines.

Use four pieces of board at least 75mm (3″) wide, and

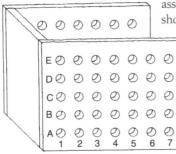

assemble them with the perforated ply to form a box, as shown in the drawing. Number and letter the holes.

Stand the box in front of the model to be copied and make sure that neither box nor model moves during measuring. A 12mm ($1/2''$) diameter dowel, marked out as a ruler, is used to measure between the box and the model. Measurements should be recorded on a sheet of squared paper.

When measuring is complete, stand the box in front of the required block of wood. Take another piece of 12mm ($1/2''$) dowel, which has a nail point projecting from the centre of one end and push it through each of the holes. This marks the wood with the same grid pattern as the box. If the design is small I ensure that the back of the carving block is flat, so that it will stand on the pillar drill. With very large designs the front of the block should be flat. The pillar drill can then have the head twisted around. Stand weights on the drill base to provide stability while drilling the holes. Holes are drilled to depths marked on the squared paper using a 12mm ($1/2''$) bit.

Removing the wood remaining between the holes is then a relatively fast process, using any manual or power tool carving method. A 25mm ($1''$) grid with 12mm ($1/2''$) holes is suitable for reasonably large scale work. It is of course possible to modify the grid and drill size according to the scale and complexity of the work being carried out.

The second copying technique which I normally use is a Dupli-Carver copying machine. This is an even faster and much more accurate system. In essence it is a related copying method. However, all measuring, marking, calculations, drilling and the inherent possibilities of error are eliminated.

Patterns for both these methods can be almost any material, such as plaster or even fabric which has had a hardener put on it. It is possible to modify the original by adding or omitting parts, or even combining different patterns into one carving.

Rod Naylor, Trowbridge , England.

3 Distorted Drawings

It's usually the case that there's this marvellous design and this great piece of wood, and they don't quite match up. You don't want to cut the wood, or perhaps you're trying to fit the design onto an already completed item of furniture, and your drawing skills aren't quite up to it.

Nearly everyone has got the message that you can change the size of a design on the photocopier at your local copy shop. But now, on the more sophisticated copier machines, width and height can be changed independently too. You can stretch or squash your drawing or illustration to fit the shape you want.

With a free form drawing, draw a frame round it to get your starting reference measurements. You will also need to know the dimensions that the drawing and its frame are to be changed to, so you may need to draw a similar frame onto the wood to get the final sizes. Armed with both these sets of measurements the percentage changes can be worked out on the copier (it is easier to do this in millimetres).

Not every operator knows what their machine can do - look for, and cultivate, the whiz kid at the copy shop. Don't make assumptions, the most skilled operator is just as likely to be the quiet little old lady as the brash teenager. Be nice to them; graphic distortion is a tricky concept to grasp. When you start with an A4 sketch and you want a final pattern 1m, (39″) high, you need someone with an organised mind at the buttons.

Frank Triggs, Shropshire, England.

4 Drawing Tips

As experienced carvers seemed to be constantly extolling the virtues of drawing a subject before carving it, I followed their advice and found pencil and paper. I also rediscovered that I could not draw, or so I thought.

I discussed my problem with a more artistically gifted friend, and she told me something that must be one of the secrets of the art world. She said that you don't need to be specially gifted to be able to draw. The sort of drawing required for carving can be learnt like any other craft, with practice, and patience, and good instruction.

She told me to start by doing outline drawings of things that I thought I was familiar with; ordinary domestic items. As I drew the familiar homely objects I started discovering how little I had actually looked at them before. I had not noticed shapes, and textures and other details.

I have kept on practising my drawing, sometimes with a carving in mind, sometimes just for the practice. I started by drawing each line two or three times in pencil until I thought that I had got it about right, then I would draw in the right line with a black felt tip pen. The resulting drawings are messy but the black lines show up the shapes I want.

Because the drawings are not for framing and putting on the wall, they only have to convey the information required for the carving; the right shapes and proportions. They are not for sale, they are working drawings.

I found that once I had adjusted my attitude to drawing, seeing it as a tool, a means to an end and not some mystic art, then I was not afraid of picking up a pencil and wasting a few sheets of paper. Has it helped my carving? I think that it has helped me to plan carvings, and to keep the proportions right, and I think I am more observant, I look at things with a more practiced eye!

P Gittings, West Sussex, England.

5 Filing

This is not an earth-shattering tip, but you may find it helpful. When I read through *Woodcarving* magazine I come across lots of bits and pieces that might come in useful 'one day'. And there are lovely photographs of carvings I might like to refer to, or I may want information from one of the tool tests.

I am sure that many have had the experience of wanting to refer to something useful from an old *Woodcarving* magazine, but having to leaf through a pile of them because we can't quite remember which one it was in. This has its uses, as I have come across things I had forgotten about. However, I find that a sticky label on the corner of the magazine cover, with page number and subjects of interest noted down, is useful for quick reference.

Vera Feldman, Birmingham, England.

6 Proportional Dividers

When designing carvings from photographs or illustrations, particularly, in my case, for walking-stick heads of animals and

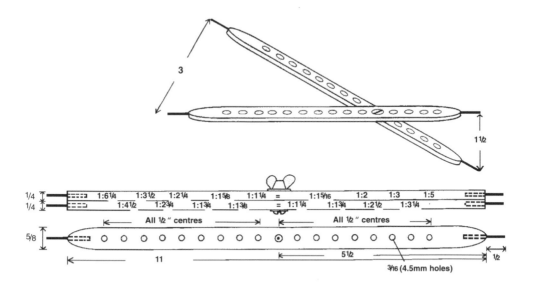

birds, I often need to enlarge or reduce the dimensions. Being unable to purchase proportional dividers, I made up my own, and find that it rapidly alters sizes without the need for tedious measurement.

Construction is simple. Cut two pieces of a hardwood 280mm (11″) long by 15mm (5/8″) wide by 6mm (1/4″) thick, and round off the ends.

Mark and drill the 4.5mm (3/16″) hole in the exact centre first, then drill one hole 10mm (3/8″) away. All the other sixteen holes are then drilled at 13mm (1/2″) centres.

Cut the heads off four hardened steel picture-hanger nails, and epoxy-glue them into pre-drilled holes in the ends, leaving 13mm (1/2″) showing - to make a total length of 306mm (12″).

A suitable bolt, two washers and a nut, or wing-nut, are used to set and clamp the dividers at any chosen ratio. These ratios can be marked on the sides of the arms, before giving two coats of sealer or varnish.

This can of course be used also as a normal divider, and I'm sure that many other carvers will find this item of great assistance in altering the dimensions of a carving pattern, to fit the size of wood available.

A.W. B. Mills, Bexhill-on-Sea, England.

7 Storing Drawings

I have developed a method of storing drawings which also enables me to enlarge them to almost any size. After making the drawing I photograph it using slide film. By doing this I can store many drawings on one slide and I am able to project them onto the wood at the most suitable size to see how they look. All you need is a camera and a slide projector.

R. Bamber , Poole, England.

8 Tracing Figures

I am quite new to carving and have found great enjoyment from copying sculptures that can be obtained from a number of sources. The difficulty is to transfer a silhouette onto a block prior to bandsawing.

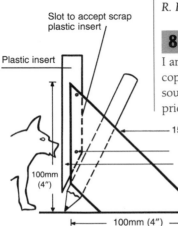

Slot to accept scrap plastic insert

Plastic insert

15mm (5/8") plywood or similar

Clearance hole for pencil

Align plastic vertically with point of pencil; drill and fix

100mm (4")

100mm (4")

I came up with the idea of this simply made instrument to overcome the problem and thought that it might help other readers.

To trace an outline, stand or lay the sculpture on drawing paper, on a flat surface. Follow the outline of the sculpture with the plastic insert while exerting gentle pressure on the pencil. The outline can then be transferred to the block - I usually cut round the outline with scissors then I can draw round it on to the block. You then repeat the process with the other elevations of the sculpture to get an all round picture.

Ted Jeffery, Essex, England.

SECTION 7 — SHARPENING

1 Buffing Veiners

This simple device speeds up the process of sharpening the inside of V-tools, veiners or any other small radius gouges.

Cut a round buffing wheel from a piece of stiff leather and mount it on the brass part of an ordinary tap (faucet) washer - this provides the spindle. Mount the buffing wheel in a drill

secured to the bench, and use sandpaper to
form a V-shaped or rounded edge on the
buffing wheel, whichever is required. Smear
the shaped edge with grinding paste and you're
ready to start polishing.

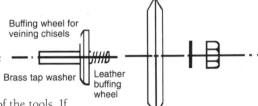

The buffing surface must rotate so that
the surface moves away from the cutting edge of the tools. If
it were to rotate towards the edge there would be a serious risk
of the tool digging into the wheel and causing an accident.

Frank Norman, South Perth, Australia.

2   Holding Water Stones

This is a tip taught to me by Toshio Odate for sharpening with
water stones. When you are soaking the stones in water place a
piece of towel in with them. When you want to use a stone put
it on the work bench on top of the wet towel. The wet towel will
hold the stone firmly in place during sharpening, without special
holding devices. After use, place both stone and towel back in
the water to soak again.

W.W. Gosnell, Chatham , Ontario, Canada.

3   Reshaped Stone

Those power carvers that use stones for detailing
feathers and fur on carvings often use a tapered
square end stone. These can be improved by
shaping the tip with a dressing stone or a
diamond disc as illustrated. I find it very easy to
control cuts, and the effect is greatly improved.
Take care when reshaping stones, and wear eye
and lung protection.

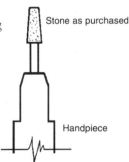

Edwin A. Leavitt IV, Gloucester, USA.

4   Sharpening Polisher

I can remember when nearly every household had a vacuum
cleaner and a floor polisher. Well the vacuum cleaners have
stayed with us, but floor polishers have fallen out of fashion -
probably due to the popularity of wall-to-wall carpets. Anyway,
old electric floor polishers can be picked up at garage sales for a

few dollars. And a floor polisher can be converted into a very good honing device.

Remove the metal fittings from two of the brushes; the fittings are usually attached by three screws. Cut out two wooden discs of the same diameter as the brushes, and cut holes in the centres to suit the metal fittings. Glue a disc of leather to the face of each wooden disc, and charge the leather with a polishing compound, such as crocus powder, or white or green buffing compound.

Turn the floor polisher upside down and locate it in a suitable spot in the workshop. I drilled a hole through the handle and attached it to the edge of a bench.

The discs spin in opposite directions and are suitable for honing both sides of knife blades; one side on each disc. Chisels and gouges can be honed on one disc.

Floor polishers usually come with an assortment of brushes, and can be adapted with sheepskin covers for polishing suitable carvings. Thick leather or felt can be glued onto discs, overlapping the edges, for polishing the flute of gouges. Abrasive cloth can also be used on discs.

It is a really simple method, that works well for a small outlay in money and time.

Don Powell, Brisbane, Australia.

5 Sharpening V-Tools

Sharpening a V-tool (parting tool or cut-off tool) seems to involve tricks that even some expert carvers don't know or use, even though they are often shown in carving manuals.

First and foremost, the cutting edges should be at right angles to the line of the tool, not rounded or laid back. Second, if you look straight on at the cutting edges, the metal is obviously thicker at the apex of the vee, so even careful sharpening will leave either a small blunt spot or a slight hook. And here is my tip, remove this blunt area by slightly - very, very, slightly - flattening the bottom of the vee. Then hone lightly inside the bottom of the vee with a suitably shaped slip stone, stroking outwards only.

The same reasoning applies in sharpening tools such as the macaroni.

E.J. Tangeman, New York State, USA.

6   Stropping Block

You can take some of the drudgery out of the grinding, honing, stropping cycle of sharpening all of your tool edges by making this gadget to mount on your lathe in a drill or on an electric motor. It is simply a turned cylinder with concave and convex sections for stropping the inside and outside edges of gouges and straight surfaces for chisels and knives.

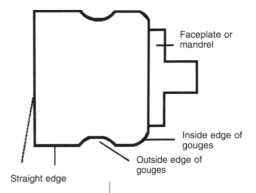

Faceplate or mandrel

Inside edge of gouges

Outside edge of gouges

Straight edge

The power stropping block is made from poplar, with approximate dimensions of 180mm (7″) diameter and 95mm (3³/4″) length. Cut the radius of the cove slightly larger than your largest gouge and the quarter radius slightly smaller than your smallest gouge.

If you don't have access to a lathe you could mount the rough sawn blank on a mandrel and rig-up a tool rest on your drill to turn it, but it may be safer to get a friend with a lathe to make it for you.

The sharpening secret is periodically charging the surfaces of the cylinder with a stick of white buffing compound. This is a fine abrasive that will leave all your tools sharp enough to shave with.

Strop a gouge by laying its outside bevel in the cove of the rotating stropping block, trailing the edge to avoid damage to the block. Roll the gouge from side to side in the cove to get the entire cutting edge. Turn the gouge over and strop the inside edge on the rounded corner of the block. Straight-edge tools can be stropped against the face of the block, or on the flat part of the circumference.

Anthony P. Matlosz, New Jersey , USA.

SECTION 8   TOOLS & TECHNIQUES

1   A Light Touch

On hard woods, particularly large sculptures, there is some need to reach areas with long bent or short bent gouges. These must be used with some caution, because they tend to spring if driven with a heavy mallet - causing stepped irregularities in the cut. The answer is to use a smaller mallet and lighter blows. Or, you could take a little longer to do the shaping by hand.

These are not problems in ordinary panel carving, so do not justify the addition of bent tools to the basic straight ones, unless you really need them. Many carvers think that more tools means better carving - golfers find to their sorrow that more clubs are not the answer.

E.J. Tangerman, New York State, USA.

2   Customised Tools

I have a tool which is a pleasure to use on long, sweeping curves, as on the model dugout canoes I carve. I made it by shortening an old aluminium-frame power door-edging plane fore and aft, and grinding the sole and the blade to a convex form. The plane's tracks closely resemble work done with a broad gouge and mallet.

For hollowing tighter curves, I soft-soldered a piece of 6mm (1/4in) brass bar on the bottom of a modelmaker's squirrel-tail plane, then filed the brass to a strongly convex form and ground the blade to suit. Hardwood epoxied in place might serve as well as the brass.

Bill Durham, Seattle, USA.

Be very careful when modifying power tools, be aware of the danger from the blades, electricity and weakening the body of the machine. If in doubt, don't do it - Ed.

3 Dental Tools

Having acquired a variable speed mini-drill the week I was due for my dental check-up it occurred to me that the very fine burrs used in dentistry would be ideal for woodcarving. I returned home from my dentist with a number of these burrs and gave them a try. They have proved to be very useful indeed in getting into tiny crevices where a conventional tool is difficult to use.

So my tip is: woodcarvers, approach your friendly dentist and ask them to save you their old drills. You'll be surprised how effective they can be - and all quite painless.

Harry Woodhouse, Lancashire, England.

4 Drum Sander

Requirements:
- Self-adhesive Velcro
- 20mm (3/4") or 13mm (1/2") rubber tap washers
- 5mm (3/16") bolts 75mm (3") long, each with two washers
- Felt backed abrasive discs - grades as required

Thread one 5mm (3/16") washer on to the bolt, followed by a number of tap washers until you have a pile of washers equal to the width of the Velcro. End with a 5mm (3/16") washer and two nuts.

Measure the circumference of the sanding drum and cut a strip of Velcro to suit, then several pieces of felt-backed abrasive to match. Stick the Velcro round the drum then an abrasive strip can be fixed to the Velcro - making sure that the join of the abrasive is not in the same place as the join in the Velcro. Tighten the first nut against the tap washers then lock it with the second nut. You are now equipped with a sanding drum.

A. Withers, Derbyshire, England.

5 Power Carving Cutters

Having read David Tippey's article on power carving cutters, I've got a tip that might help some carvers.

There is a very wide range of cutters designed for the goldsmiths' trade with a shaft diameter of 2.34mm (0.092") (can't figure that in fractional inches), and jewellers' suppliers should be able to deliver them. There are cylindrical cutters (1-8mm), cone shaped (with different angles), ball ended (0.5-10mm), hollow (0.8-5mm inner diameter), inverted cones, flame, bud, oval, vee, knife edge and hubs, and more.

One address in Germany - they deal internationally - is Karl Fischer GmbH, Berliner Str. 18, Postfach 567, -75105 Pforzheim, Germany.

Markus Ellermeier, Idar-Oberstein, Germany.

6 Punches & Frosters

Commercially produced punches don't always produce the desired effect, so it is often necessary to file the ends of lengths of rod, or perhaps a 152mm (6″) nail, to the shape required. Two punches that cover a large number of requirements are a frosting punch and a dome punch.

A frosting punch or froster is made using a short length of sharp hacksaw blade, about 13mm (1/2″) long. This is glued with epoxy resin into a slot hacksawn into the end of a length of rod - teeth outwards of course. Frosting tools like this are traditionally used to texture backgrounds in relief carving, but they can also be used to indicate stitching, or horse harness or clothes for example.

For a dome punch a shallow hole is drilled in the end of a length of rod. By moving the drill from side to side as the drilling proceeds a spherical hollow is formed. When the rod is pressed into the wood it will leave the impression of a sphere. I find this useful for quickly forming eyes - a pointed punch forming the centre of the eye. It can also be used for making the centre of flowers, or it can form decorative geometric patterns.

Margaret Elliott, Cornwall, England.

7 Reducing the Shock of Carving

Other arthritis-prone carvers may find this tip useful, as they could be faced with a similar dilemma. Five years ago I was confronted with the choice of further injections in my right elbow joint, or give up woodcarving. Shock was being imparted to my right elbow by mallet blows when carving, and this was irritating my arthritic joint. Not wishing to have to give up my woodcarving, I bought a small panel-beater's mallet, with a solid rubber head (it cost 95p). I shortened the handle to a comfortable 'grip-hold', and have successfully used it instead of a conventional carving mallet ever since.

However, at present I haven't been able to avoid injections into my left wrist, despite employing a loose grip when holding chisels and gouges. I would appreciate any suggestions to reduce the jarring effect, which aggravates the condition.

Another tip - this time to avoid wear and tear on my arms, while sorting through my piles of old magazines. If an article, tip or advert attracts my attention I note it in a loose-leaf file; putting details under specific headings, along with the magazine issue and page number. This saves a lot of time and frustration when I want to re-examine the article later on.

Patricia Vardigans, Northamptonshire, England.

A solution to the problem of protecting the left hand from mallet shocks may be to slip a length of water-pipe insulating foam over the handle of your chisels and gouges. The foam is available to fit several diameters, and can be bought cheaply in one or two metre lengths. It could be attached temporarily by binding it in place with string, and if it proves effective, it could be glued in place with PVA adhesive - Ed.

8 Versatile V-Tool

Most carvers only use a V-tool for incising v-shaped lines and marking the borders of a pattern for setting in, cleaning up corners, texturing, squaring up and so on.

It is also particularly good for creating a shallow vertical edge. If the tool is tilted slightly so that the edge against the design is vertical, then the outside edge of the cut can be smoothed away with a firmer. In some crafts this is called fairing. The vertical edge will appear to be above the faired edge.

This technique is valuable in creating an illusion of greater depth in bas-relief carving and in carving a woven-textured effect.

E.J. Tangerman, Port Washington, USA.

Using a V-tool for 'fairing'

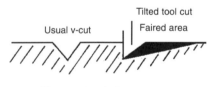

Woven-textured effect

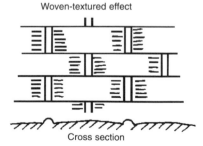

Cross section

Avoid Breakage

A major cause of tool breakage, particularly in tough woods like ash, is the tendency of a driven tool to stick in the cut. It is not the fault of the wood or the tool, the problem lies with the carver.

In most cases the tool has been driven in too deeply, then the carver becomes impatient and tries to wedge, pry or twist the tool to get it loose. It's no wonder that the tools break; thin tools, like v-tools and small chisels, are hard tempered steel and are not pry bars.

If a tool won't roll out of the cut sideways, a chip must be cut cleanly on all edges so that the tool can be removed without levering. Cut away wood around the tool's stuck edge and pull it back out in the direction it was jammed in.

E.J. Tangerman, Port Washington, USA.

SECTION 9   VICES & WORKHOLDERS

1   Alternative Carvers' Screw

The Test Report on woodcarvers' screws in the March/April 1994 issue of *Woodcarving* was incomplete, without the inclusion of a reference to lag screws as an alternative.

Galvanised lag screws in assorted sizes and diameters can be acquired for approximately 30 cents a screw. They resist corrosion, and I am certain have superior holding power. An appropriate wrench can be acquired for approximately five dollars.

This is a cheaper, stronger, and more versatile alternative in my opinion. I assume similar tools and screws are available at similar prices in the UK.

Robert C. Acheson, New Port Richey, USA.

Lag screws are available in the UK, but are not easy to find - Ed.

2   Gentle Grip

Often you will reach the stage of a project when you need two hands for the carving operation, but the piece is too delicate or

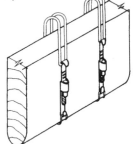

too awkwardly shaped to be gripped in a vice.

My solution uses two medium size worm-drive hose clips. Saw them in two, bend the sawn ends back to form u-shaped hooks, and you have two adjustable tensioning devices. When used with soft cord loops, these tensioners will hold the project firmly to an oddment of timber which can then be gripped in the vice. If necessary, soft packing can be inserted between the timber and your carving.

Customised hose-clips and soft cord used to hold awkward or delicate pieces

I devised this method during my pattern-making days, when I found it necessary, but almost impossible, to gain a firm hold while carving the complex shapes of intricate control valve bodies.

W. Brian Taylor, Milnthorpe, Cumbria.

3   Holding Jig for Relief Carving

I have found this jig very useful on many occasions for holding medium to large relief carvings.

The baseboard can be plywood or chipboard, about 12-20mm thick ($1/2''$-$3/4''$). This is screwed to a tenon of about 100mm x 50mm x 150mm (4" x 2" x 6"). The tenon can then be held in an ordinary carpenter's vice or Workmate. This will allow a degree of pivoting.

The relief carving is laid on the baseboard and four triangular pieces of any scrapwood cut about 75mm x 75mm (3" x 3") depending on the size of carving. These are placed evenly around its outside and screwed to the baseboard.

A space is left between the carving and the bottom two triangles to admit two wooden wedges. When these are lightly tapped into position they hold very firmly indeed. The idea can be varied to suit almost any shape of work.

F.B. Howkins, Haslemere, England.

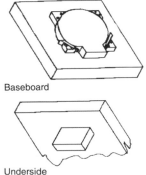

Baseboard

Underside showing tenon

The most difficult part of carving birds seems to be the feet. Most carvers buy cast feet which are expensive and need selecting to suit each particular bird.

4 Jig for Bird Feet

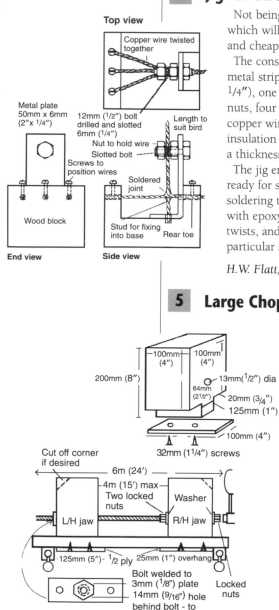

Top view

Copper wire twisted together

Metal plate 50mm x 6mm (2" x 1/4")

12mm (1/2") bolt drilled and slotted 6mm (1/4")

Nut to hold wire

Slotted bolt

Screws to position wires

Soldered joint

Wood block

Stud for fixing into base

Length to suit bird

Rear toe

End view   **Side view**

Not being overflushed with cash I have made a jig which will produce legs and feet for any bird quickly and cheaply.

The construction is very simple and consists of a metal strip 140mm x 50mm x 6mm (5¹/2" x 2" x 1/4"), one 75mm x 12mm (3" x 1/2") bolt and three nuts, four screws 20mm x 6mm (3/4" x 1/4"). It uses copper wire from offcuts of electric cable with all the insulation stripped off. These are twisted together to a thickness to suit the bird.

The jig enables the various pieces to be positioned ready for soldering, which becomes very easy. After soldering the feet are removed, trimmed and covered with epoxy putty which adheres perfectly due to the twists, and can be shaped as required to suit each particular species of bird and method of mounting.

H.W. Flatt, Cambridge, England.

5 Large Chops

100mm (4")   100mm (4")

200mm (8")

13mm(1/2") dia

64mm (2¹/2")

20mm (3/4")

125mm (1")

100mm (4")

32mm (1¹/4") screws

Cut off corner if desired

6m (24')

4m (15') max

Two locked nuts   Washer

L/H jaw   R/H jaw

125mm (5") - ¹/2 ply   25mm (1") overhang

Bolt welded to 3mm (¹/8") plate   Locked 14mm (9/16") hole   nuts behind bolt - to clear studding

When I needed temporary carver's chops to hold a rather larger carving than usual - a rocking horse - I proceded as follows: I cut two jaws from 100mm x 100mm (4" x 4") oak (an old gate post) each 200mm (8") long, cut a rebate 20mm (3/4") wide, by 25mm (1") deep at the bottom, then screwed and glued 100mm x 125mm (4" x 5") pieces of 13mm (1/2") ply using two 32mm (1¹/4") x 10 screws per jaw.

A 13mm (1/2") diameter hole was drilled 115mm (4¹/2") from the top of each jaw to take a 610mm (24") long rod of 12mm (1.3") threaded studding. A 19mm (3/4") bolt is welded on at each side of the right-hand jaw (or pairs of nuts locked together) and another bolt is welded to a 3mm (1/8") plate screwed to the outside face of the left-hand jaw.

Mount the chops in a Workmate, and tighten the Workmate jaws on to the right-hand jaw only of the chops, leaving the left-hand jaw free to slide. Use a 19mm ($3/4''$) socket wrench and ratchet-handle from car tool-kit, to wind the left-hand jaw in, to grip work-piece firmly. Then tighten Workmate jaws on to left-hand chops jaw, providing a very firmly held workpiece.

The top inside edges of the jaws can have cork or padding glued on, if necessary, and the top corners of jaws are chamfered or rounded off. Total cost - about £4.00, rather less than carvers chops at about £120!

A.W.B. Mills, Bexhill-on-Sea, England.

6 Modified Workholder

I have been using this addition to my workholder for some time now and found it very useful. It uses two sets of sash-cramp heads (the sort you can buy to make your own sash-cramps with), some 50 x 25mm ($2'' $ x $1''$), timber and a base board.

The size of the base board and the length of the rails can be made to suit different sizes of carving or relief panel. I have two different sizes made up and just swap the cramp heads over.

J.R. Benham, Surrey, England

7 Relief Carving Workholder

As a newcomer to woodcarving, and with a limited budget for tools, I tried using a Black & Decker Workmate as a bench. This I found to be too low, and not very convenient for holding the relief carving that I was working on. So, I set about building a jig to solve both of these problems.

The jig was built from scrap materials, so all dimensions should be taken as guidance only. The work-surface 520mm x 420mm x 32mm ($20^1/2''$ x $16^1/2''$ x $1^1/4''$) is a piece of kitchen worktop, with four batons 40mm x 20mm ($1^5/8''$ x $3/4''$) screwed around its edges. These should be fitted at right-angles to one another, but with gaps at the corners to allow woodchips to be brushed out.

Underneath, the work-surface is fitted to two pieces of deal 400mm x 90mm x 40mm ($16''$ x $3^1/2''$ x $1^5/8''$), using screws countersunk into its surface. Two further pieces of deal 750mm x 65mm x 40mm ($29^1/2''$ x $2^5/8''$ x $1^5/8''$) are long enough to

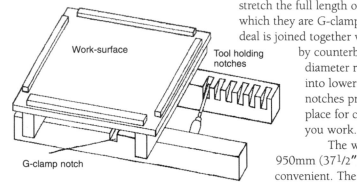

Work-surface

Tool holding notches

G-clamp notch

stretch the full length of the Workmate top, to which they are G-clamped at the notches. The deal is joined together with 63mm (2¹/2″) screws by counterboring a 12mm (¹/2″) diameter recess (1⁵/8″) 40mm deep into lower members. The sloping notches provide a convenient resting place for chisels and gouges while you work.

The working height is raised to 950mm (37¹/2″), which I find quite convenient. The workpiece can be set into one corner without clamping, provided that all carving is done working into the corner. This way the workpiece may be turned very quickly, to allow carving in any direction. For delicate work it will be necessary to wedge the workpiece in position. One possible method uses battens and wedges, allowing the work to be released and turned very quickly.

Derek Andrews, Bedford, England.

Two wedges, driven in vertically. Made to suit size of work

Squared battens, size to suit the work

Method of wedging workpiece in frame   Wedge angle about 5°

8 Simple Support

Many carvers use elaborate vices, clamps or workholders for carving in the round. For supporting small three-dimensional hand-sized pieces, something that I find works well is a small bag filled with sand, kitty litter, or other small hard grains (even dried beans). The work is held down on the bag, so that the section being carved is supported. The bag moulds itself to irregular shapes as you carve.

My bag is about 150mm (6″) square, made of soft leather. In twenty years of use I have only had to patch three holes with tape.

E.J. Tangerman, New York State, USA.

9 Slippery Customer

To hold a curved half log, sawn surface uppermost, and keep the
bark undamaged, I constructed a shallow box that held the
wood with its top surface sticking out. I wrapped the lump in
cling film, and with a stiff brush, forced it into every cranny of
the bark. I placed the wrapped wood into the shallow box and
filled the remaining space with a pour of plaster of Paris. The
plaster set, I was able to carve the exposed surface; clamps
holding the box. To remove it the box was cut into quarters.
Next time I shall extend the bottom of the box to form clamping
lugs.

Ken Barnes, Berkshire, England.

10 Stop Carvings Sliding

To stop woodcarvings sliding around the workbench I use a piece
of anti-slip carpet underlay. This is a sticky feeling plastic mesh
used underneath mats and carpets to stop them 'walking'. A piece
underneath a carving is almost as good as gluing it to the bench,
but it is much easier to adjust to get in the right position.

Also, if you cover the top of a Black & Decker Workmate
with the underlay you can saw large items without them moving
- the mesh holds work almost as well as clamps, without the
fiddle of clamping up.

I have found sticky carpet underlay available in two sizes,
800mm x 1500mm (31$^1/2''$ x 59″) priced about £4.50 and
1300mm x 1800mm (51″ x 71″) at about £8.50, from Ikea
stores, though it is probably also stocked by other carpet shops.

Valerie Knott, Northampton, England.

WOOD    SECTION 10

1 A Wood Patching Tip

Sawdust filled epoxy cement is perhaps the best of all possible
wood patches, especially for use under epoxy or urethane
varnishes. This makes a rigid patch that can be formed with
abrasive carving tools, so it is good for carving projects as well
as for furniture projects.

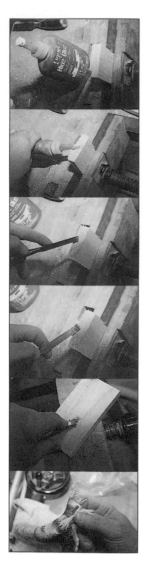

If all you need is small amounts, this patching material can be made by the same method as I learned years ago from master carver Chris Effrem, though his method used commercial liquid hide glue rather than epoxy. His theory was that since even the best planks you're likely to find have some minor imperfections in them and as the cost of hardwoods keeps rising, cutting around these minor flaws becomes less and less desirable and artful patching becomes more and more desirable.

Stick shellac is good, but it's also fragile and never quite the right colour, and blending tones can be messy, time consuming, and not very precise. None of the various putty, wood dough, or 'plastic wood' products seem suitable for more than the most ordinary applications; they too have colour matching problems, and, like the shellac sticks, they don't take finish in quite the same way as regular wood. If there were an alternative that was both superior and readily available, you'd think someone could make a (woodworker's) fortune with it. No one has. So, what would you say if I told you that you already have the key ingredients to a superior wood patching compound in your shop, that it will always match your project perfectly, and that it will always be fresh because you make it only as you need it.

Here is how he made it:

The materials you need are extremely simple. Buy a small bottle of liquid hide glue; this works better than does the hot hide glue you might make from crystals and water, for it sets rather more slowly. Buy small bottles, so that you work with fresh glue more often. That's the only thing you should need to buy, for the other ingredient is the cut-off from the board that requires the patch. By all means, experiment with the hot hide glue for those applications where you're really pressed for time; hot hide glue will work just fine if you really hustle.

Set a cut-off of the material you're patching in the vice on your work bench, end-grain up. Put a drop of liquid hide glue on the end-grain. With a very sharp chisel, but not one of your best chisels, scrape the end-grain, through the glue, in strokes a couple of inches long. Alter the scraping strokes enough to thoroughly mix the fine shavings you raise with the glue. When the mixture of glue and 'dust' reaches the texture your experimenting demonstrates to be most useful to you, apply it to the damaged area with the chisel. My photos don't really do a very good job of illustrating the texture, but I find that I get best results when I blend the material so that it is somewhat thicker than commercial wood dough.

It's important to work neatly; after all, your goal is to repair an imperfection, not to make a mess with glue and dust. After the glue has set, this patch will sand and finish nicely. Hide glue does less to prevent the finish from working than do the more readily available PVC woodworking glues.

As I mention potential problems and their solutions, it's important to note that some woodworkers do this sort of thing with white glue and the contents of their belt sander's dust bag. Don't use that for other than the crudest work; the dust in your belt sander's bag includes small abrasive particles which are certain to ruin your finish, and, unless your clean-up is absolutely meticulous, the white glue is sure to show up under almost any finish. Besides, the micro-thin 'scraped' shavings are the perfect consistency for this application, as these shavings are more like flour than dust. If you must use a plank other than a disposable cut-off, be certain to clean the end off, or to cut off enough so the piece isn't out of square when you get ready to use it in a project. This step is almost as important as cleaning and lightly oiling or waxing the chisel. Cleaning up the plank and the tool while the material is wet is much easier than chipping off chunks of dried glue.

This is a useful technique for inexpensive patching. Even if you already have a satisfactory method for doing this, this one is worth experimenting with...there's no telling when having another 'trick' like this will save your project.

Hugh Foster, 848 N. 6th St., Manitowoc, WI 54220, USA.

2 Bamboo Dowels

I am a dabbler in most forms of woodwork, from Anthony Dew-type rocking horses, through joinery work to carving, the last being my favourite form of woodwork. As a hobbyist, I tend to use small pieces of timber, as I can afford the time to build it up into such widths as I need. So this is the subject of my tip.

All the books say that, when joining boards with glue, you should tap a couple of brads into one surface then nip them off

Alternative positions while glueing

Pointy end
(or cut a point if need be)

Straight through

Angled

As a dowel

Rubber band
during glueing

with pliers to stop the pieces sliding. That works fine mostly. Then when you come to saw or carve the laminated piece, sure as God made little apples, that is where the cut will be made. The result is a gapped chisel or a blunted saw blade.

Again, when in a delicate part of a carving it is necessary to use a brad or a thin nail in lieu of a dowel where the grain line changes abruptly - and two pieces have to be glued at or near a rightangle - one is apt to have trouble either by reason of hitting the hidden nail or adhesion difficulties.

Then it is time to look at the humble bamboo Satay stick (Shishkebab stick) and mentally turn it into a dowel. As Chris Pye's article on butterfly carving points out, he uses this sort of bamboo for antennae because of its enormous cross grain strength, even when thinned down. Yet it is as kind as wood to cutting tools. Also, it has miniature built-in glue release slots. So these little sticks are marvellous dowel material. They come in a few thicknesses (in Australia they do anyway) to suit fitting to 2mm (3/32"), 2.5mm (7/64") and 3mm (1/8") holes. For anti-sliding devices, nip off a short length, drill a hole, and leave the pointy end up for a few millimetres. Then tap the second board on top. Or, if you have a little waste, simply bore straight through into the second board.

The second major usage - as a thin dowel - is as for any other sort of dowel. I've found that boring a hole straight up through what will be, for example, the thin leg of a water-bird carving is also another use. But this requires a longshank small drill (not always easy to come by), and a bit of good judgment.

I hope I have promoted the use of the world's tallest grass - bamboo, thereby saving trees... and chisels!

Clive Price, 76 Burns Parade, Chapel Hill , Queensland 4069, Australia.

3 Clean-Edged Holes

I wished to insert a circular eye in a convex carving, but when I started drilling a provisional hole the edge of the hole began splintering down the grain. So, I turned a piece of mild steel to the required outside diameter, to suit the eye. I then reduced the diameter of the first 6mm ($1/4''$) to act as a pilot in the previously drilled hole. The face of the larger diameter was recessed at about 45 DEG to create a cutting edge round the complete circumference.

The pilot was positioned in the previously drilled hole, and tapping on the tool cut through a circle of fibres; I used a skew chisel to remove the wood in the circle. The process was repeated until the required depth was reached.

This technique produced a clean accurate hole, that retains the eye without the aid of glue.

C.J. Brown, Barnstaple, England.

4 Curing Common Complaints

The frustrations that woodcarvers experience while following their craft can cause so much exasperation at times that many must almost give up. Two of the most common recurring problems I have encountered, during 15 years carving, are thin section breakage, and stress cracks in the wood. Both seem to occur at the final stages of the chisel, or the rough sanding work. The steps I take to cope with these problems have been developed down the years.

Thin sections that are close to the danger limit are items such as birds' beaks and legs, fingers, noses, ears, and so on. I have found that a few drops of wood hardener, which can be bought from most hardware stores, will penetrate up to 6mm ($1/4''$) and dries overnight to give a solid consistency that can be carved like marble. The wood doesn't have the same consistency as before and will clog abrasive paper, but it will have a good finish and is stronger. Drying cracks, or stress cracks I ignore until I have almost finished the sanding, then I do the cosmetic work. I have to prepare for this problem right at the start of a project by taking shavings with a bench plane of a variety of thicknesses. I use the plane on several sides to allow for variations in the colour of the wood. The shavings are flattened with a steam iron, and stored until needed. If any cracks have shown up in the carving, I sand an area 6mm (1/4″) either side of the crack then cut a piece of wood shaving slightly longer than the crack, the grain running along the crack. The shaving is glued in place with a cyanoacrylate superglue that sets in seconds; it is then carefully sanded. If the colour and grain have been carefully selected, the patch is almost invisible.

James Hare, Dumfries, Scotland.

5 Hiding Cracks

Many large logs have checks (shakes or cracks) from drying stresses. In some cases these checks occur at very undesirable places in a carving. The usual remedy is to attempt to push in a glue and sawdust mixture, which usually doesn't penetrate.

I have found it better to put the glue on alone, work it down into the check with a thin-bladed knife, then sprinkle the area with sawdust and work that in turn. The result is a crevice that is more deeply filled.

Larger breaks or imperfections in the wood should be filled with pieces of the same wood, carefully fitted, because a sawdust-filled hole of any size will have a different colour, even before finishing. I usually make such repairs with a filler piece cut carefully from a chip of the same colour and grain direction as the wood around the flaw.

E. J. Tangerman, New York State, USA.

6 Plum Dead

An old plum tree was blown down in the garden a few years ago, and I thought that it would be a useful supply of free carving wood. The trunk was about 300mm (12″) diameter at its widest, and about 1525mm (60″) long. My local timber yard told me that they would machine it, but that I would have to pay for transporting the trunk to the sawmill.

This started to make my free wood get expensive, so I

decided to try and convert the log myself. I don't have a large bench saw or bandsaw, and felt the hand sawing the log would be too much, so I decided to use wedges to split the log. Mike Abbott explains this ancient technique in his book *Green Woodwork*, and I had seen oak trees that had been riven in this way at the Anglo-Saxon village in West Stow, Suffolk. I used a steel wedge to make the initial split in the end of the log, then 'chased' it along the length of the log with hardwood wedges, made of beech and oak off-cuts. I had to use a handsaw to cut the pieces to length.

The technique was very successful, cheap, and not too difficult. I was limited to the dimensions and shapes of the pieces created this way, but I have a number of carvings and bowls in the lovely red-brown wood from our plum tree.

Leo Rudge, Somerset, England.

7 Prevent Cracking

To prevent baulks of wood stock from developing ruinously deep shakes and cracks, I bore a few deep holes (where wood will later be removed in carving) with a 50mm (2″) Forstner bit while the wood is green. This seems to relieve stresses and to promote even drying until I am ready to begin carving the piece.

Bill Durham, Washington, USA.

8 Wood Hardener

Previous tips have mentioned various ways of hardening patches of soft fibrous or thin wood. I use the fast-drying cyanoacrylate adhesive 'Hot Stuff' for this job. I have used it on items thin in section, such as flower petals or feathers, and within 15 seconds it is firm enough to proceed with additional carving or handling without damage.

W.W. Gosnell, Ontario, Canada.

1 Changing Letter Size

Illustrations of letters are available from a variety of sources, but they are rarely the size you need. If the size of your letters is not exactly that required for your inscription, you can easily enlarge or reduce them, without resorting to a photocopier.

The angle between the stems of such letters as A, K, M, V, W, Y and Z is constant for each letter, regardless of its size. This fact can be utilised to change the size of each letter.

When you have decided where the letters are to go, draw in the parallel lines of the top and bottom of the letters.

Using a bevel gauge, or an adjustable protractor, align the long arm along the bottom of the letter in the sample copy. Look directly down over the letter and adjust the other arm of the gauge until it lies along the imaginary centreline of the letter's stem. You may find it easier to draw in the centrelines on your sample alphabet.

Without altering the setting of the gauge, transfer it to the corresponding place on your layout on the wood. Draw in the centreline, stopping slightly short of the top and bottom lines to allow for the serifs and the width of the letters. Move the gauge to each side of the centreline and draw in the outer edges of the letter stem. These lines can now be used as starting points for the adjoining letter stem.

You will probably find that the angle obtained by using this method differs from that of your roughly chalked layout lines. Don't alter the angles you've just taken from the sample alphabet - erase the chalk and adjust the rest of the inscription. If you start changing the angles of letters to suit the layout it will look awful. The angles must be consistent - for instance all the Ws must look the same.

Be prepared to spend time getting things right and looking good. You may even have to alter the size of the letters again.

Zoë Gertner, Somerset, England.

2 Letter Spacing

It is most important to get the layout and spacing of lettering right before you start carving, as it is difficult to re-space letters once you have cut two or three.

One very useful method I have used for laying out lettering

is to use rub-down letters, such as Letraset. These letters are available in a wide range of styles and sizes, they can be quickly applied, and are easy to remove if the lay-out proves to be unsatisfactory. Once correctly positioned they provide an excellent guide for carving the letters, and they have no blunting effect on tools when you cut through them.

David Place, Shrewsbury, England.

3   Lettering Layout

When initially laying out an inscription for carving I find it best to roughly draw the letters using chalk - to assess their placement and spacing.

Chalk can easily be removed with a damp cloth and letters, words and spacing can be simply adjusted so that the inscription is visually pleasing, and correct when viewed from a distance.

When the layout is correct it can be redrawn more accurately using a pencil.

Zoë Gertner, Somerset, England.

FINISHING   SECTION 12

1   Brush Work

How many of us carvers treat our glue brushes with the same loving care as we lavish on our chisels?

For years I used worn-out soggy brushes for my work when gluing up unexpected splits or replacing chips, even though they slosh glue on the parts of a carving where you don't want it.

Then one day I spotted a pig-bristle fan brush in an art shop. As its name suggests, this has stiff bristles shaped like a fan. Its broad surface area means it can hold lots of adhesive for large pieces. However, it is also very thin in profile and the bristles are stiff enough to be thrust deeply into narrow splits. You can even use the brush to force the split a little wider to get the glue right down to the end.

And by looking after it, one brush has given me years of service.

Clive Price, Queensland, Australia.

2 Cleaning up Glue

These two tips especially apply if you are having to fix bits to a carving towards the end of a project - gluing wings on a bird or perhaps repairing cracks. Glue marks from early stages are usually carved away.

Many books and magazines recommend that we clean wet PVA adhesive off our projects with a wet rag. This smeared adhesive then dries in the grain and seals the wood; any finish subsequently applied won't penetrate the glue-sealed area, leaving an odd looking patch.

I have long recommended that the adhesive is left to dry until it is slightly harder than dry cottage cheese, then it can be removed with a very sharp chisel. After removing glue this way, and taking a couple of passes with a cabinet scraper, there is much less likelihood of the glue showing through the finish.

A different approach when gluing up panels is to let the glue dry hard then take a quick pass at it with a No. 5 gouge. This is followed by a few strokes with a Stanley Surform plane. This looks good, is comparatively easy and as well as removing adhesive the process flattens slightly mismatched panels.

Hugh Foster, Wisconsin, USA.

3 Faster Drying Oil Paints

When painting sculptures I often use oil based paints, but instead of using linseed oil as the medium I use Danish or tung oil. Linseed oil is both a traditional wood finish and an established medium for oil paints, however it is a very slow-drying oil. Tung oils are inherently faster drying, and Danish oils are essentially tung oil with additional resins and dryers. As a result I find that if I use Danish oil instead of linseed oil with oil paints, the finish can be handled more quickly and is slightly more durable. The brushes clean up with white spirit in the normal way.

If you are painting carvings that are to be toys, please make sure that the paints are safe for this purpose. Small children instinctively put things in their mouths, and although it may take a great deal of paint to take effect, none of us would like to feel responsible for the sickness of a child. In Britain - and the rest of Europe – paints for toys are covered by British standard

BS 5665, which is the same as the European standard EN71, so if the blurb on the side of the paint container says that the paint conforms to these standards it is safe to use.

Paddy Adams, Somerset, England.

4 Home-Cooked Filler

To fill up a small hole in wood, mix coffee powder, starch and water together to form a thick paste.

Fill in the hole, smooth with a damp finger and wipe with a dry cloth.

Debbie Wilcox, Birmingham, England.

5 Natural Stand

When carving long-legged birds such as waders, I use soft iron wire of the right thickness for the legs. This is easy to bend into the appropriate positions and can be ground to a sharp point at both ends for fixing. I fix them into the body first and then the stand.

To create a natural-looking stand, I look for branches that have been broken off in the wind or stumps of trees that have been felled. These are often left with a rough edge of largish splinters. Once I have made the stand the desired shape, the sharp ends of the legs can be pushed into drilled holes among the splinters. What would have been the feet are completely hidden. The result is perfectly natural, as if the bird were walking among reeds or grasses.

John Payne, Kirkby Lonsdale, Lancashire.

6 Storing Mixed Acrylic Paint

I am sure I am not alone in experiencing great difficulty in achieving the exact colour mix that I want when working with acrylic paints. I am a wildfowl woodcarver and the right colour is important.

It is therefore all the more frustrating to find that having achieved the right colour, the paint on the palette has dried out before the painting is finished.

I have found that a Rowney's Stay-Wet palette, with its plastic dish and semi-permeable membrane, works reasonably well but is expensive at over £5. I prefer to use my own solution to the problem of drying out.

Quite simply, I put the mixed paint, ready for use and before dilution, into a 35mm film cassette container, taking the precaution to label it. With the lid tightly in place that paint will remain in a perfectly usable condition for many weeks or even months and the paint can be used as often as you wish over that period. The containers will cost you nothing; just go to Boots or wherever films are accepted for processing and they will be only too glad to be rid of them.

Jim Pearce, 12 Roughwood Close , Watford.

INDEX